RECORDING THE BLUES

ROBERT M.W. DIXON and JOHN GODRICH

STEIN AND DAY / *Publishers* / New York

First published, in both hard cover and paperback editions, in the United States of America by Stein and Day / *Publishers* / 1970.

Printed in England
Stein and Day / *Publishers* / 7 East 48 Street, New York, N.Y. 10017
SBN 8128-1318-9 (hard cover)
    8128-1322-7 (paperback)

Produced by November Books Limited
Designed by Ian Cameron
House editor: Elizabeth Kingsley-Rowe

*The illustrative material for this book
has largely been taken from record company catalogues and publicity material
for the period covered as well as from
record labels, mainly reproduced specially from the originals for this book.
Most of the illustrations are from
material in the collections of the authors
who are grateful to Peter Brown for
lending the label reproduced on page 79;
to Paul Manners for that on page 33; to
Bob Yates for the catalogue on page 8;
to Albert McCarthy for the photograph
on page 20; and to Paul Oliver for
the illustrations on pages 14, 62 (right)
and 75.*

CONTENTS

FOREWORD

Early in 1920 the General Phonograph Corporation issued, for the first time, popular songs performed by a black girl. The success of this record made the industry aware of a vast, untapped market: black Americans were eager to buy records by artists of their own race. Two or three record companies immediately began systematic recording of blues singers, gospel quartets, and the like, numbering the discs in special series that came to be called 'Race Series'. They sold so well that other companies entered the field and soon every blues singer who had ever appeared on a theatre stage had also made her contribution in the recording studios. The companies began to look further afield. Many made field trips to the south, recording itinerant rural blues singers, guitar evangelists and shouting black preachers. By the late 'twenties these 'Race Records' – which sold to an entirely black market – were about as far removed as is possible from white America's popular music of the day.

Gradually, the style of race records changed. In the 'thirties, when more and more of the black audience had migrated to northern cities, they preferred performances by urban musicians – with a full rhythm section laying down a strong beat – to the more delicate guitar-only accompaniments of country singers. Blues and pop moved closer together during the 'forties and 'fifties; today it is often difficult to distinguish them. Records that are now normal pop fare would have been considered blues performances, for a strictly minority audience, twenty years ago.

Pop music has drawn on blues material, on tunes and styles that were featured in the race series. In this book we examine the content of these race series during the period 1920–1945; the ways in which the companies discovered talent, how they recorded the singers and how they marketed the records. We deal only with blues and gospel records, leaving aside instrumental jazz, novelty numbers, and other items that from time to time appeared in the race series.

BIRTH OF AN INDUSTRY

Thomas A. Edison's first phonographs, in 1877, were novelties; people paid to hear an approximation of their own voice played back to them at a phonograph exhibition. It was not until 1888 that instruments were manufactured in quantity, for home entertainment; and musicians and celebrities began to be lured into the studios, to record their talent for posterity. Edison established the North American Phonograph Company to handle sales, and this in turn set up thirty regional subsidiaries. The most promising of these was the Columbia Phonograph Company, covering Maryland, Delaware and the District of Columbia. Although the parent company failed, Columbia prospered, partly due to its exclusive contract with John Philip Sousa. By the turn of the century two companies were competing for the expanding market in phonographs and cylinders: Columbia and Edison's new National Phonograph Company.

But there was competition from another quarter. The National Gramophone Company had, since 1897, been manufacturing disc records. Through astute management, and because of the greater appeal of the flat record, discs were soon gaining ground on cylinders. By purchase of a vital patent, Columbia were also able to begin manufacture of discs, in 1902.

In 1901 the National Gramophone Company was reorganised as the Victor Talking Machine Company. It was, and remained, the undisputed leader of the industry. In 1902 Victor issued records by actors, music-hall entertainers and after-dinner speakers, as well as by the great opera stars of the day. In that year it also issued six single-sided records by the Dinwiddie Colored Quartet, a group that sang in a quite authentic Negro style, without the European influence that marked the work of other early gospel groups, such as the Pace Jubilee Singers. It was to be eighteen years before another recording of authentic black music appeared on the market.

Victor and Columbia controlled all the patents for lateral recording, in which the needle moved from side to side in the groove. When Edison, faced with a dwindling market for cylinders, decided to enter the disc business in 1912, he had no choice but to make 'hill-and-dale' records, in which the needle moved vertically in the groove, as on cylinders. Hill-and-dale records

QUARTETS—MEN'S VOICES

Negro Shouts by DINWIDDIE COLORED QUARTET

These are genuine Jubilee and Camp Meeting Shouts sung as only negroes can sing them.

1714 **Down on the Old Camp Ground**
1715 **Poor Mourner**
1716 **Steal Away**
1724 **My Way is Cloudy**
1725 **Gabriel's Trumpet**
1726 **We'll Anchor Bye and Bye**

Page 42 of the 1903 Catalogue for Victor Talking Machine Records also listed the Anvil Chorus and Selections from Iolanthe.

could not be played on Victor or Columbia gramophones; anyone who bought an Edison gramophone could only buy Edison records for it. Columbia ceased manufacture of phonograph cylinders in 1917 but Edison continued until his company finally discontinued making records of all types, in 1929.

Pathé-Frères, the leading European manufacturer of cylinders and records, began recording and issuing discs in America in 1914. In 1915 the General Phonograph Corporation – financed by the Lindström Company, a successful German record concern – issued discs on the OKeh label. And in 1916 the Aeolian Company, who had been manufacturing gramophones for two or three years, began the Vocalion label. All these new companies had to be content with producing hill-and-dale records.

In 1915 the Starr Piano Company of Richmond, Indiana, decided to enter the record market. Hill-and-dale discs issued between 1915 and 1918 – first on the Starr label and then on Gennett – sold badly. Who was going to buy records that could not be played on Victor or Columbia machines? In 1918 Starr produced lateral-cut discs, and Victor immediately brought suit for patent infringement. In the subsequent protracted litigation Starr were supported by, amongst others, the General Phonograph Corporation, the Aeolian Company, and the Canadian Compo Company, who all stood to gain if Victor's patent were upset. Eventually, the Supreme Court pronounced in favour of Starr. Any company was now free to make lateral-cut records.

THE NEW MARKET 1920-1922

A few items by black performers had been issued in the early years of recording but they were intended for white audiences. These minstrel routines and orchestrated spirituals generally reinforced the traditional image of the Negro.

But black citizens were increasingly buying talking machines, and with them recordings by the white artists of the day. In January 1916 the *Chicago Defender* – a weekly newspaper with a circulation of a quarter-of-a-million, that reached black communities in all parts of the country – commented that its readers had, in the course of their Christmas spending, 'paid to hear Tettrazini, Caruso . . . But how many of our race ever asked for a record of Mme Anita Patti Brown, Mr Roland Hayes, Miss Hazel Harrison, Miss Maude J. Roberts, Mr Joseph Douglas . . .?' The *Defender* campaign intensified; in October 1916 they announced that 'records of the Race's great artists will be placed on the market' once the record companies had ascertained 'how many Victrolas are owned by members of our Race'. Each black owner of a talking machine was asked to send his name and address to the *Defender* office. But the *Defender* did not mention the matter again, and no records by black concert artists were forthcoming.

When the breakthrough came it was from a quite different direction. In 1920 Fred Hager of the General Phonograph Company, who had started issuing lateral-cut discs on the OKeh label the previous year, wanted to record *That Thing Called Love* and *You Can't Keep A Good Man Down*, composed by Perry Bradford, a black music-store proprietor from Chicago. Hager had intended to use Sophie Tucker but Bradford eventually persuaded him to use Mamie Smith, a black girl. The tunes were recorded on the second Saturday in February and issued on OKeh 4113 in July 1920. The record was listed as 'Mamie Smith, Contralto' in the catalogue and OKeh made no attempt to draw special attention to it. But the black press proclaimed 'Mamie made a recording' and sales were unexpectedly high. Mamie was called back to the studio in August to record *Crazy Blues* and *Its Right Here For You (If You Don't Get It . . . 'Tain't No Fault Of Mine)*. This time OKeh advertised widely in black communities and when the disc was issued in November it was an instantaneous success. OKeh had tapped a vast potential market – tens of thousands of black enthusiasts were willing to pay $1 each (a considerable sum by the standards of the day) to buy a record by a black singer. It may not be coincidental that the first record by a black concert artist – Mme Anita Patti Brown – was cut in September of that year.

The other companies were not slow to notice the success of *Crazy Blues*. In 1921 Emerson featured two blues records by Lillyn Brown, while Pathé-Frères issued four by Lavinia Turner on their Pathe and Perfect labels, and Starr one by Daisy Martin on the Gennett label. Recordings by coloured singers were being issued at an average of about one per week during 1921 and 1922. In January 1922 *Metronome* declared that 'every phonograph company has a colored girl recording blues'.

Although the *Talking Machine World* of 13th October 1920 bore an advertisement for Mamie Smith, now an exclusive OKeh artist, describing her as 'singer of "Blues" – the music of so new a flavor', she was in fact more of a pop singer. And there was in any case nothing new about blues – Ma Rainey had been stomping the south for a dozen years, singing the most classic of blues. In November 1920 Arto, a small company from Orange, New Jersey, recorded a popular light-skinned singer named Lucille Hegamin. *The Jazz Me Blues* and *Everybody's Blues*, accompanied by Harris's Blues and Jazz Seven, released in February 1921 on Arto Universal Record number 9045, could be considered the first real blues disc. Retailing at 85 cents, it sold well, but the great hit of the year was Miss Hegamin's follow-up: *I'll Be Good But I'll Be Lonesome* – a promise to be faithful during a lover's absence – and *Arkansas Blues*. The latter had trite words:

> Ain't got no time to lose
> I'm tired and lonely, I'm tired of roaming
> I long to see my mammy in my home-in . . .
> I've got the Arkansas blues

but the catchy tune, the vibrant jazz accompaniment by the Blue Flame Syncopaters (spelt thus) and the singer's bluesy, syncopated style combined to produce a performance that was hard to resist. Despite Arto's poor standard of recording other companies fell over each other to lease the masters and the Hegamin version

Lucille Hegamin and her Blue Flame Syncopators.

of *Arkansas Blues* was eventually issued on eleven different labels. OKeh called Mamie Smith into the studios in early September to record her own version of *Arkansas Blues*, issued on OKeh 4445.

Arto issued six records by Lucille Hegamin in 1921, and three in the early months of 1922. But despite her success the company was failing and went into bankruptcy in 1923. Lucille had been signed to a one year's exclusive contract by the Cameo Record Corporation on October 4th, 1921. Cameo produced a cheap 50-

cent record and they put out a new Hegamin disc every other month until 1926. In fact this was almost all they did issue for the black market – of the twenty-six blues records released by Cameo over a four-year period twenty-three were by Lucille.

Of the major companies, only Victor stood aloof from the blues craze. They had heard and rejected Mamie Smith in January 1920, and Lucille Hegamin (singing *Dallas Blues*) in October. Victor decided to concentrate on trying to sell its prestigious Red Seal classical records to Negroes. The other major company, Columbia, could not afford to ignore any new market; they had overproduced in 1921 and were heavily in debt. Columbia signed up Mary Stafford, a cabaret artist, and she recorded *Crazy Blues* in January and *Arkansas Blues* late in September 1921. Six Mary Stafford records were issued in 1921 but her contract was not renewed, Columbia turning to Edith Wilson the following year. During this period Columbia showed little initiative, trailing behind the

other companies and having no inclination to break new ground or issue more than just one blues disc every other month. Indeed it is said that after Mamie Smith's *Crazy Blues* became a hit, a Columbia executive heard Mary Stafford singing the song in a Harlem cabaret; she was recording it in the Columbia studio the next morning. The story may be an exaggeration but it is certainly true that at this period the companies made little effort to seek out good or new talent. They relied on contacting singers who happened to be performing in the New York area or, in many cases, on the singers contacting them.

In January 1921 Harry Pace left the Pace and Handy Music Company, in New York, to form his own company, the Pace Phonograph Corporation. It began with a staff of one clerk in a small basement room. In May, Pace announced his Black Swan records, which would feature only coloured artists and be produced by a company all of whose stockholders and employees would be coloured. He stated, 'Black Swan records are made to meet what we believe is a legitimate and growing demand. There are 12,000,000 colored people in the U.S. and in that number there is hid a wonderful amount of musical ability. We propose to spare no expense in the search for and developing of the best singers and musicians among the 12,000,000.' Bandleader Fletcher Henderson was engaged as musical director and recording manager and one of the first three records issued was by singer Katie Crippen, accompanied by Henderson's orchestra. It has been suggested that the label name was derived from a coloured singer called Elizabeth Taylor Greenfield, who was known as 'the Black Swan'.

Pace was critical of other concerns which only recorded blues numbers by black artists; he announced his intention of covering the whole range of 'colored performances' – including quartets, glee clubs, vaudeville acts and concert singing. But, economically, Pace was forced to fall back on blues. Ethel Waters was paid $100 for her *Down Home Blues* in mid-1921. This, together with *How Long, Sweet Daddy, How Long* by Alberta Hunter, is said to have pulled the company out of the red. By October, Black Swan announced that they had 'moved to larger premises, employing fifteen clerks, an eight-man orchestra, seven district managers, were represented by 1,000 dealers and agents throughout the country and were shipping 2,500 records from their plant each day to as far afield as the Philippines and the West Indies.' By the end of 1921, Pace had signed Ethel Waters to a contract, stipulating that she did not marry within the year, which was said to make her the highest paid coloured recording star in the country. It was announced that $104,628 had been paid for Black Swan records in the past eleven months.

On Friday, 20th January 1922, a blues singing contest was held in the Manhattan Casino, New York, as part of 'the 15th Infantry's First Band Concert and Dance'. Four singers were featured: Miss Lucille Hegamin, 'Harlem's Favorite' singing *Arkansas Blues*, Miss Alice Leslie Carter with *Decatur Street Blues*, Miss Daisy Martin with *If You Don't Believe I Love You* and 'The Southern Nightingale', Miss Trixie Smith who was pronounced winner and presented with a silver loving cup for her own composition *Trixie Blues*. Harry Pace signed the winner and soon released *Trixie's Blues* on Black Swan 2039, the singer's high-pitched, infectiously rhythmic vocal admirably backed by a small anonymous jazz group:

> Now if you don't want me, daddy, you have no right to lie,
>   hey, hey
> Now if you don't want me, that's no right to lie
> 'Cause the day you quit me, daddy, that's the day you die

April 1922 was an important month for Black Swan. Harry Pace, in partnership with one John Fletcher, purchased the Olympic Disc Record Company. The Olympic plant was now used for pressing

Right: Harry H. Pace of Black Swan Records. Altogether 43 records appeared in Black Swan's 14100 series, including some of their most successful blues.

Black Swan records, and items by white singers from the Olympic catalogue were reissued on Black Swan – thus breaking Pace's pledge to use only black artists. Black Swan stepped up releases from three to ten a month, and reduced the price of its popular records to 75 cents. They also introduced comic, hillbilly and operatic Red Label series. A Red Label release, by a coloratura soprano of the Chicago Grand Opera, Antoinette Garnes, was advertised as 'The First Grand Opera Record Ever Made by a Colored Singer';

it sold for $1. Maybe because he felt a little ashamed of breaking his 'all-black policy', in August Pace began a new 14100 series restricted, with one exception, to black singers, and featuring mainly blues items. However, the records cannot have sold quite as well as Pace had anticipated for in December 1922 he advertised 'Exchange your old, worn or damaged phonograph records for new Black Swan Records at Kelly's, 2289, Seventh Avenue. 15 cents allowed on records of any make, on each new record purchased', and by April of 1923 Black Swan were appealing 'We Want Live Agents Everywhere! Music stores, drug stores, furniture dealers, news stands, cigar stores, manicuring and hairdressing parlors, confectionary stores, shoe shining parlors, delicatessen shops and all other places of business catering to retail trade . . .'

There were several small record ventures at this time. Over in Los Angeles, black music-store proprietors Johnny and Reb Spikes began an 'all-colored' label called Sunshine in June 1922. Only three issues appeared – one each by blues singers Roberta Dudley and Ruth Lee, accompanied by Kid Ory's Jazz Band, and an instrumental by Ory. The music was recorded in the west, 5,000 copies of each issue were pressed over in the east and these were then shipped back and sold over the counter of the brothers' own shop in Los Angeles. It was to be more than twenty years before any further blues recordings were made on the west coast.

In March 1922 the black vaudeville team of Thomas Chappelle and Juanita Stinnette produced six records, five of which featured themselves, on their own label C & S Records; after this no more was heard of the company. The same year W. C. Handy, the black composer and Pace's erstwhile partner, decided to form his own record company and advertised two items in the *Chicago Defender*; however, none seem to have appeared. And in March '22 there was an advertisement for Echo Records – the name being more-or-less OKeh reversed – which was said to be 'a new concern owned and operated by the Negro people. Shelton Brooks, Lucille Hegamin, Lena Wilson and other stars will record for the Echo as soon as their present contracts expire . . . agents are wanted everywhere.' But, as far as is known, no Echo records were ever issued.

OKeh, who had unwittingly started it all, continued to be leader of the new trend. Mamie Smith continued to be featured (twenty-three more Mamie Smith records were issued by OKeh in 1921 and 1922) and in the early months of 1921 other, more bluesy, singers were summoned to the OKeh studios. In the summer of

1921 General Phonograph became the first company to issue a special brochure describing releases by black artists. It listed six records: a new Mamie Smith, unaccompanied singing by the Norfolk Jazz Quartet, two discs by Tim Brymn's Black Devil Orchestra (including an instrumental version of *Arkansas Blues*), and the first records by blues singers Daisy Martin and Gertrude Saunders. OKeh advertisements toted the special 'colored supplement' but they did not draw attention to the fact that, although the Mamie Smith and Norfolk Jazz Quartet discs bore numbers in the general 4000 series (these items being perhaps expected to sell to white as well as to black customers), the other four records were numbered 8001 to 8004 in a special series that was to be reserved for black talent. In fact it was January 1922 before OKeh drew attention to the new series: new releases 8018 to 8020 were then advertised 'for the Colored Catalog'.

A name was needed to describe records intended for black consumption, but there was no obvious term. The description 'colored records' was used most frequently in advertising in 1921. In January 1922 the OKeh advertisement in the *Chicago Defender* said 'All the greatest Race phonograph stars can be heard on OKeh records' and in March they invited readers to 'ask your neighborhood dealer for a complete list of OKeh race records'. But 'race', a term of common identification used within the black community, was not yet the recognised name; the word was not mentioned in OKeh advertisements during the remainder of the year. Then in May 1923 OKeh announced 'The World's Greatest Race Artists on the World's Greatest Race Records' and thereafter the term was used regularly in *Defender* advertising. It had taken almost two years to evolve a name for the 8000 series. Even so, OKeh were for a while cautious about using the name in all contexts – their advertisement in the *Talking Machine World* in August 1923 mentioned the company's 'Negro records'. Soon, however, 'Race Records' became, within and without the industry, the established name for black records intended for the black market; it remained so for twenty years.

OKeh had issued forty records in the 8000 series by the end of 1922 – half-a-dozen jazz instrumentals, eleven records by male quartets, and a couple of dozen blues discs by Daisy Martin, Gertrude Saunders, Josephine Carter, Esther Bigeou and a singer from New Orleans, Lizzie Miles (they also put one of Mamie Smith's couplings into the race series – all other records by Mamie were put out in the general series until she was dropped by OKeh,

at the end of 1923). With the demise of Arto, Black Swan was the only serious competitor for the race market, and that company was beginning to find itself in financial difficulties. But in 1922 a new and powerful rival emerged.

The Wisconsin Chair Company of Port Washington was interested in all types of home furniture and it was a natural step, a few years after it had begun production of phonographs and cabinets, to form a subsidiary to manufacture records. The New York Recording Laboratories began issuing records on the Paramount label in 1917. Their initial blues releases were Lucille Hegamin's first two hits, which were leased from Arto and numbered 20052 and 20053 in the Paramount popular series, in mid-1921. Early in 1922 they recorded *Daddy Blues* and *Don't Pan Me* by Alberta Hunter, who had had two records released on Black Swan the previous year, and when the record was issued in mid-'22 it was numbered 12001, the first disc in a special Paramount series that was to be reserved for black talent. The series was priced at 75 cents, but Paramount's advertisement in the *Defender* contained a special offer: five records – the first three in the 12000 series, 20151 by Lucille Hegamin and 20143 by Specht's Society Entertainers – for $3. By then OKeh had reduced their price to 75 cents – the standard sum charged for 10-inch records by Victor, Columbia and the other major companies throughout the 'twenties. The Paramount race series started slowly – only nine records were issued in 1922 – but by 1923 it was competing fiercely with OKeh. OKeh described its 8000 series as 'The Original Race Record' and Paramount responded by dubbing the 12000 series 'The Popular Race Record'.

The companies were reaching wider and wider audiences with their race releases; a November 1922 OKeh advertisement listed twenty stockists outside New York: four in Chicago, three in St Louis, two each for Detroit, Cleveland and Pittsburg, and one in each of Milwaukee; Wellesville, Ohio; Indianapolis; Knoxville, Tennessee; Poor Fork, Kentucky; Lexington, Kentucky; and Bessemer, Alabama. It was becoming obvious that the fifty blues records per year issued during 1921 and 1922 went nowhere near satisfying the demands of the market.

Left: Alberta Hunter, 'The Idol of Dreamland', recorded prolifically for Black Swan, Paramount, Gennett, OKeh and Victor; her accompanists ranged from a white studio band to Louis Armstrong and Tommy Ladnier.

THE CLASSIC BLUES 1923-1926

In 1923 race records came into their own. OKeh and Paramount were putting out an increasing number of records, and just about every other company began searching for black talent. In 1923 and 1924 blues and gospel items were being issued at an average of four per week. The figure increased to five a week in 1925 and went up again the following year; more than 300 blues and gospel discs appeared on the market in 1926. These were the years of the classic blues singers – professional vaudeville and cabaret performers, almost exclusively female, who sang 12-bar blues interspersed

with a few traditional and pop numbers. Sometimes their accompaniment was just a pianist but often it was a small hot jazz band. Altogether race records were issued on more than fifteen different labels during this four-year period. However, three companies – OKeh, Paramount and Columbia – dominated the market and together accounted for more than two-thirds of the total blues and gospel releases.

The main event of 1923 was the emergence of Columbia as a major race label. Frank Walker, a white impresario who was an enthusiast for both hillbilly and blues, had heard Bessie Smith singing at a gin-mill in Alabama several years before. When Walker was put in charge of Columbia's race list the first thing he did was to send for Bessie, one of the most popular singers of classic blues in the south. At first Walker played safe, getting Bessie to record numbers that were already well-known through the recordings of other singers. Her first disc, recorded in New York in February 1923, featured *Down Hearted Blues* – already selling well on Paramount 12005, by Alberta Hunter – and the second coupled *Aggravatin' Papa* with *Beale Street Mamma*, selections that were on Cameo 270, by Lucille Hegamin.

After a four-line introduction, *Down Hearted Blues*, on Columbia A3844, goes into the traditional 12-bar form, Bessie's voice rich, deep and clear over Clarence Williams's piano accompaniment. The memorable final verse:

I've got the world in a jug, the stopper's in my hand (*twice*)
I'm going to hold it until you men come under my command

and the power of Bessie's singing combined to make it a hit. Bessie was soon back in the studios, recording her own material; and indeed Lucille Hegamin was called by Cameo in August to make her own version of *Down Hearted Blues*, in the hopes of cashing in on some of Bessie's success. Bessie Smith was soon established as the biggest selling blues artist of the period; many consider her to be the greatest blues singer of all time.

At the end of June, Walker recorded another fine singer – Clara Smith (no relation to Bessie). Clara's voice was thinner than Bessie's but she had a delicacy and feeling that made her records sell only slightly less well than Bessie's. In 1922 Columbia had issued seven blues records; in 1923 they put out three dozen,

Photograph: 'The Empress of the Blues', Bessie Smith.

including fourteen by Bessie and eight by Clara. Towards the end of 1923 Columbia decided to number race records in a special series – 13000D and 13001D were by Bessie Smith, 13002D was by Clara. But this series was scrapped after eight issues – through fear of the unlucky number thirteen influencing sales – and just before Christmas the 14000D series was begun (naturally enough, with a record by Bessie Smith).

Although Columbia's race catalogue was flourishing, the company found it impossible to extricate itself from its financial troubles. Bankruptcy was acknowledged in 1923 and the company was then run by a consortium of bankers, its biggest debtors. The pattern set in 1923 was maintained over the next three years. Blues and gospel releases averaged about three per month in 1924, and increased to four each month in '25 and '26. Monthly advertisements in the *Chicago Defender* in 1923 gave way to weekly insertions the following year. In 1925 everybody's advertising increased; like its main rivals – OKeh and Paramount – Columbia had a dozen full-page advertisements in the *Defender* that year. But, under the conservative policy imposed on the company by the bankers' consortium, there was little attempt to diversify the race list – with Bessie and Clara's records making up half the total number of releases it was essentially a two-artist catalogue.

Matching Columbia's fourteen records by Bessie Smith, in 1923 Paramount issued twelve by Alberta Hunter and OKeh no less than seventeen by a new singer, Sara Martin. In 1923 there were too many record companies chasing too few singers: eleven artists each had more than six records issued that year, between them accounting for more than half the total releases. The best singers were under contract to one or other of the three big companies. Lesser performers made the best of the situation, recording for whoever would have them – and almost everyone would. In 1924 Rosa Henderson had records issued on six different labels – Vocalion, Ajax, Perfect, Brunswick, Emerson and Banner (and this was no isolated instance: Lena Wilson came out on six in '23, Hazel Meyers on six in '24, and Edna Hicks on no less than seven different labels in '23). More talent was urgently needed, and OKeh and Paramount were out to find it.

The 1924 Paramount catalogue bore a picture of J. Mayo Williams, black recording manager for Paramount's 'Race Artist Series.' In a paragraph headed 'What does the public want?' Paramount asked 'What will you have? If your preferences are not listed in our catalog, we will make them for you, as Para-

Photograph: J. Mayo Williams.

mount must please the buying public. There is always room for more good material and more talented artists. Any suggestions or recommendations that you may have to offer will be greatly appreciated by J. Mayo Williams, Manager of the Race Artists Series.' Williams lost no time in signing well-known but previously unrecorded artists. In 1924 a Paramount advertisement bore a large headline 'Discovered at Last – "Ma" Rainey'. In the 1924 catalogue she was described thus: 'Recognised as the greatest

blues singer ever known. Her records are breaking all records for popularity. "Ma" is the Mother of the Blues, because she really taught many of the younger stars how to sing Blues.' Most notably she had trained Bessie Smith, who as a girl had toured with Ma in the Rabbit Foot Minstrels show. Ma Rainey was to be a mainstay of the Paramount 12000 series for the next seven years.

When, in May 1924, Paramount decided on a promotional

stunt, it centred on Ma Rainey. Ma Rainey's sixth release –
numbered 12200 – was labelled *Ma Rainey's Mystery Record*; the
performance was said to be so moving that no one in the Paramount
offices could think of a suitable name for it. Prizes of phonographs
and records were offered for the most apt title, to be judged by
Mayo Williams and Harry Pace. The winning entry was *Lawd,
I'm Down Wid De Blues* by Ella McGill of Jefferson, Indiana –

but the labelling on the record was never changed.

In 1923 Paramount issued just over fifty blues and gospel items (their advertisements claimed 'A New Hit Record Released Every Week'), half-a-dozen or so more than OKeh. Then in April 1924, when Black Swan's financial position became impossible, it was taken over by Paramount; numbers 12100/99 in the Paramount race series were reserved for reissue of Black Swan material. The newspaper announcement talked of a 'merger' but the details made it clear that Black Swan had had little option: 'The Black Swan catalogue of several hundred master records is the most valuable of its kind in existence. Instead of the company operating that catalogue, the Paramount company will manufacture and distribute Black Swan records, from which the Black Swan Co. will receive a definite amount each month. After the Black Swan Co. has paid its accounts and obligations, such as every operating company must have, it will be in a position to pay its stockholders a substantial and continuous dividend, or it can retire its capital stock at a substantial premium.' It was a sad end for the only company with 'all colored stockholders' but Black Swan assured the Race that 'by Black Swan's combination with the Paramount company – a white organisation devoted to the interests of the Race and specializing in Race records – the continuance of high class Race music is assured.' By and large, Black Swan's confidence in Paramount was justified. Mayo Williams was constantly on the lookout for new talent that could be brought to Chicago to record. Unlike the bigger companies – who sold exclusively through record stores – Paramount did a good mail order business. Every advertisement and supplement had a triangular blank at the bottom; all one had to do was tick the records required and fill in one's name and address – and then pay the postman 75 cents per selection. There must have been a good chance that if there were some marketable singer or band of whom Paramount had never heard, then some rural customer would scrawl a recommendation on the back of the order slip.

In addition to digesting Black Swan, Paramount issued an average of almost four new blues and gospel discs a month in 1924; the next year it was just over five a month and this figure was maintained through 1926. But OKeh was the market leader during the classic blues period. Each year the company issued twenty more blues and gospel items than it had the previous year until in 1926 just over a hundred new records were released. Eighty or so were classic blues in the finest tradition – including

Sara Martin, the vaudeville team of Butterbeans and Susie, Alberta Hunter (who had been dropped by Paramount in 1924) and two singers from Houston, Texas: Sippie Wallace and the teenage Victoria Spivey. In June 1926 OKeh organised an 'OKeh Race Record Artists' Ball' in Chicago, featuring half-a-dozen of their most popular singers, in addition to the bands of King Oliver, Louis Armstrong, and many others; the *Chicago Defender* produced an extra 'Music Edition' to celebrate the event.

Ralph Peer, son of a white Missouri storekeeper, was in charge of the 8000 series and he was always on the lookout for new talent. In 1923 Polk Brockman, a white man who was OKeh's wholesale distributor in Atlanta, persuaded Peer to bring his equipment to Atlanta to record Fiddlin' John Carson, a favourite hillbilly singer. The June 15th edition of the *Atlanta Journal* advertised Peer's visit, and by the time a makeshift recording laboratory was set up in an empty loft on Nassau Street quite a lot of local talent had assembled. The *Chicago Defender* gave news of the trip, saying that Peer had made a 'record by Lucille Bogan, a popular blues singer from dear old Birmingham, Alabama, and an original blues by Fannie Goosby, amongst others.' OKeh 8079 coupled Lucille Bogan's *Pawn Shop Blues* with *Grievous Blues* by Fannie Goosby, the first race record to have been recorded outside the main centres of New York and Chicago. Lucille Bogan was called to New York almost immediately to record four more titles, and Miss Goosby followed a month or two later. At the end of 1923, OKeh advertisements were able to boast not only that 'OKeh made the first 12-inch blues Race record' (by Eva Taylor, one side being *Gulf Coast Blues*, a 'cover' of one of the tunes on Bessie Smith's first record) and that 'the first duet record by colored artists was on OKeh' but also that 'new OKeh Race Artists have been discovered by special recording expeditions into the South.'

Peer visited each of Atlanta, New Orleans and St Louis several times during the next few years, primarily to record hillbilly talent, but he normally also recorded one or two blues singers at each location. Polk Brockman was the talent scout in Atlanta and would advertise in the local paper and scour the countryside looking for likely talent, which he would audition himself, ahead of the arrival of the OKeh unit. Brockman claimed that he would often go to a town and find 200 people waiting to see him. In St Louis, Jesse Johnson, black proprietor of the De Luxe Music Shop and husband of blues singer Edith Johnson, was talent scout at various times for a number of companies including both OKeh and Paramount. Field trips were well advertised: in May 1926 Victoria Spivey's brothers, hearing that OKeh were to be in St Louis, sent their sister there, to audition for Jesse Johnson. Two or three days later she recorded four tunes for the OKeh field unit (including the haunting *Black Snake Blues*). These were so successful that she was called to the New York studios in August; OKeh issued six Victoria Spivey discs that year.

During the classic blues period, the three major companies advertised extensively. They would describe the content of the record, the qualities of the singer, the exceptional dedication of the company – all in the most lowdown imitation-jive-talk prose. A full-page Columbia advertisement in the *Chicago Defender* for 19th July 1924 said 'Wow – but Bessie Smith spills fire and fury in *Hateful Blues*, on Columbia record 14023D'. The smaller print went on 'Talk about hymns of hate – Bessie sure is a him-hater on this record. The way she tells what she is going to do with her "butcher" will make trifling fellows catch express trains going at sixty miles an hour. The music is full of hate too. You can almost see hate drip from the piano keys. Fury flies off the violin strings. Every note is a half-note. No quarter for anyone.' And above a list of other Columbia releases the copywriter declared, 'Having a phonograph without these records is like having pork chops without gravy – Yes, indeed!' A full-page OKeh advertisement in the 1925 *Defender* lauded Sippie Wallace, 'The Texas Nightingale': readers were invited to 'catch those Sippie Wallace notes as they float sky high or deep down low. Hear her as she sounds those ice cold words with their red hot meaning. Do it now with her up-to-the-second OKeh blues, "He's The Cause Of My Being Blue", on OKeh.'

In 1921 Victor had auditioned at least four black singers before deciding not to issue any blues records for the time being. With the expansion of the race market in 1923 – and Columbia's great success with Bessie Smith – Victor could no longer afford to remain aloof. Serious recording commenced in April 1923 and Victor's first three blues issues were numbered 19083 to 19085 in the popular series – they advertised 'A Special List of Blues' in the *Chicago Defender* during August. But the best singers were under contract to OKeh, Paramount or Columbia and the artists Victor were able to secure – Rosa Henderson, Edna Hicks, Lena Wilson, Lizzie Miles – were not in the same class as Bessie and Clara Smith, or Ida Cox, Paramount's new star. It may have been

poor sales, or perhaps some general change in company policy, that caused Victor to cease blues recording as suddenly as they had begun. The last session involved Gertrude Saunders – who had had a single record in the OKeh 8000 series in 1921 – on Monday, 27th August 1923. Victor had issued seven blues records in 1923; they did not release a single selection for the race market during the following two years.

Thomas Alva Edison, who still confined himself to cylinders and hill-and-dale discs, was finding times increasingly hard. In 1923 he issued two blues records by Helen Baxter and in 1925 he put out a batch of three race records – 51476 to 51478 – by Rosa Henderson, Viola McCoy and Josie Miles. Four blues titles even found their way on to Edison's Blue Amberol cylinders. But Edison's next race release was not until 1929 – Eva Taylor singing *Have You Ever Felt That Way?* and *West End Blues* – issued just a few weeks before the company discontinued all record production.

After the conclusion of Gennett's successful battle in the courts with Victor in 1921, a close friendship arose between them and

OKeh, Aeolian-Vocalion and Compo due to their support in the fight. This led to a pooling and leasing of Gennett and other masters, which was later extended to other companies, such as Paramount. Also part of the arrangement was that H. S. Berliner of Compo would make pressings for Gennett and the others in Montreal.

At first Gennett did not appear to see eye-to-eye with the

Below: Gennett's main studio, in Richmond, Indiana. Recording had to stop whenever a train went by outside.

general trend towards race records and this may well have been an important factor in their steadily declining sales in the early 'twenties. Although they conceded the Daisy Martin record in 1921, they didn't enter the market proper until 1923, with twenty issues by such minor singers as Viola McCoy, Edna Hicks and Josie Miles. Gennett's interest (or the public's interest in Gennett's choice) appeared to wane again after this and an average of less than one blues record a month was maintained until the end of 1926, with little of note among them. Gennett records originally sold for 75 cents – maybe even 85 cents in 1921 – but when their

3000 series appeared in 1925 the price was cut to 50 cents, probably in an effort to boost sales. Recordings alternated between their studios in Manhattan, and Richmond, Indiana, where the pressing plant was situated.

Ajax records, first advertised as 'The Superior Race Record' and later 'The Quality Race Record', made their appearance in October 1923 and sold for 75 cents. They were manufactured in Canada by the Compo company in their Lachine, Quebec, plant. Ninety percent of Ajax records were by black artists and the blues masters were specially recorded for them in New York and marketed through the Ajax Record Company of Chicago. By August 1925 they had disappeared from the scene, but at least 136 records had been issued over a period of two years, including items by Rosa Henderson, Viola McCoy, Monette Moore (under the pseudonym Susie Smith), Mamie Smith and their own exclusive artist Helen Gross.

Late in 1925 another black record company was promoted, this time in Kansas City by the singer and entertainer Winston Holmes, who had his own music store on 18th Street. Meritt records sold at 75 cents and were pressed in batches of 400 according to demand; they only achieved seven issues in three years. Lottie Kimbrough's *City Of The Dead* and *Cabbage Head Blues*, labelled as Lena Kimbrough, was Meritt's best seller, closely followed in popularity by two sermons from Rev J. C. Burnett, *The Downfall Of Nebuchadnezzar* and *I've Even Heard Of Thee*. These so appealed to Columbia that they persuaded Burnett to record for them; Holmes sued for breach of contract, but lost. The Winston Holmes Music Company finally went out of business about 1929.

The Aeolian Company issued just over two dozen race records on its Vocalion label in 1923 and 1924 – by minor artists, such as Lena Wilson, Viola McCoy, Rosa Henderson and Edna Hicks, who went the rounds of the smaller companies. Towards the end of 1924, Aeolian's record division was bought by the Brunswick-Balke-Collender Company of Chicago (BBC) – makers of billiards and bowling alley equipment – who had issued half-a-dozen discs by exactly the same group of artists on their own Brunswick label in the autumn of '23 and the spring of '24. There was little race activity at BBC in 1925 – six or so issues on the Vocalion label and none at all on Brunswick. Then in March 1926, BBC announced the formation of a Race Record Division, which would be headed by Jack Kapp, formerly Columbia's representative in Chicago.

2204-A
THE WELL OF SALVATION
Rev. H. C. Gatewood, D.D.I.M.R.A.
and The Faithful Worshippers
(509)

WINSTON HOLMES MUSIC CO. KANSAS CITY MO

The Vocalion 1000 series – the fourth major race series – was inaugurated the following month. BBC tried to develop an image for the new series; reacting against the *double-entendres* of many current songs, they announced 'Better and Cleaner Race Records', a description that was retained until May 1928. Two dozen blues records were issued before the end of the year – as well as a fair amount of jazz – but they were mostly by the minor classic blues singers (those that had not been snapped up by the main companies). It was an uninspiring start for the new series.

Between 1923 and 1926 the great majority of blues records were by women, professional singers who sang mostly for city audiences, using fairly standard song material. There were exceptions: in 1924 OKeh issued two tunes recorded in Atlanta, *Barrel House Blues* and *Time Ain't Gonna Make Me Stay* by Ed Andrews, accompanying himself on his own guitar. However the record cannot have been a great success, for Andrews never made another.

Then, late in 1924, the Paramount talent scouts brought in Papa Charlie Jackson, a minstrel show entertainer who accompanied himself on the banjo. His first record – *Papa's Lawdy Lawdy Blues* and *Airy Man Blues* on Paramount 12219 – sold well, and Paramount's batch of releases for the New Year of 1925 included Papa Charlie's second record: the traditional *Salty Dog Blues* backed with *Salt Lake City Blues* (Papa Charlie's woman has left him and he declares he's going to jump on a freight train and go to Salt Lake City where 'you have a wife in the morning, another wife at night'). Papa Charlie had eight records in the 12000 series in 1925 – only Ida Cox and Ma Rainey had more – and was one of Paramount's most successful artists for a further five years. In 1927 a Paramount advert asked 'have you heard about the twitching, twisting, shaking, shimmying, throbbing, sobbing – sensational new dance, "Skoodle Um Skoo"? Papa Charlie Jackson, the one and only "Papa Charlie", tells about it in his latest Paramount record. Its a torrid record with some mean banjo picking with it. Ask your dealer for Paramount 12501 or send us the coupon.'

Paramount, because of their mail order service, had more rural customers than the other companies and some of these were requesting recordings by country blues singers. In 1925 Sam Price – later to become a well-known race artist in his own right, but then working in a music store in Dallas – wrote to Mayo Williams recommending Blind Lemon Jefferson, a rough itinerant singer and guitar-picker from Texas. He was at once called to Chicago; Paramount – overall a smaller company than OKeh and lacking the justification provided by an extensive hillbilly catalogue – made no field trips to the south. Blind Lemon's first two selections, on Paramount 12347, were *Booster Blues* and *Dry Southern Blues*:

> The train's at the depot with the red and blue lights behind
> (*twice*)
> Well, the blue light's the blues, the red light's a worried
> mind

They were unlike anything that had appeared on record before. Blind Lemon's expressive, whining voice and his fluent guitar – complementing and sometimes replacing the voice – were an unbeatable combination. Paramount issued eight records by Lemon in 1926 and he was their major artist for the rest of the decade. Realising the demand for country blues performers – men who, unlike the classic blues singers, wrote almost all their own material – Paramount began looking for more talent of this type. In September 1926 they recorded Blind Blake from Georgia, a slightly more sophisticated performer whose records sold almost as well as Lemon's. Observing Paramount's success with Blind Lemon and Blind Blake, other companies were soon recording country blues, and in the closing years of the decade were competing as fiercely for this new market as they had over the classic blues singers a few years before.

In 1925 Bell laboratories perfected the technique of electric recording, and the rights to this new process were offered – at a highish price – to Victor and Columbia. But the consortium controlling the bankrupt Columbia company was reluctant to make so heavy an investment. English Columbia, which had been owned by the American company until 1922, had a go-ahead management who were determined to secure rights to electric recording. When it turned out that this was only possible through an American

My Lord's Gonna Move this Wicked Race

A wonderful, inspiring, spiritual song that will never grow old. Beautifully rendered by the perfectly blended voices of the famous Norfolk Jubilee Quartette. It's a song that is sure to inspire you. Everyone who hears it will feel uplifted—just a little bigger and better in heart and spirit. Every Christian home will prize this record.

12035—MY LORD'S GONNA MOVE THIS WICKED RACE Vocal Quartette
Norfolk Jubilee Quartette
FATHER PREPARE ME Vocal Quartette   Norfolk Jubilee Quartette

PARAMOUNT JUBILEE SINGERS

12072—STEAL AWAY TO JESUS Mixed Quartette Paramount Jubilee Singers
MY SOUL IS A WITNESS TO MY LORD Mixed Quartette
Paramount Jubilee Singers
12073—WHEN ALL THE SAINTS COME MARCHING IN Mixed Quartette
Paramount Jubilee Singers
THAT OLD TIME RELIGION Mixed Quartette
Paramount Jubilee Singers

ELKINS-PAYNE JUBILEE SINGERS

12070—STANDING IN THE NEED OF PRAYER Male Quartette
Elkins-Payne Jubilee Singers
I COULDN'T HEAR NOBODY PRAY Mixed Quartette
Paramount Jubilee Singers
12071—GONNA SHOUT ALL OVER GOD'S HEAVEN Male Quartette
Elkins-Payne Jubilee Singers
DOWN BY THE RIVERSIDE Male Quartette
Elkins-Payne Jubilee Singers

MME. M. TARTT LAWRENCE

12092—HIS EYE IS ON THE SPARROW Piano Acc.   Madame Lawrence
STAND BY ME Piano Acc.   Madame Lawrence

MME. HURD FAIRFAX

12040—I'M SO GLAD TROUBLE DON'T LAST ALWAYS Mezzo Solo, Piano
Acc.   Madame Hurd Fairfax
SOMEBODY'S KNOCKING AT YOUR DOOR Contralto Solo, Piano Acc.
Madame Hurd Fairfax

→→ ────────────────BLACK SWAN────── ←←
THE RACE'S OWN RECORD

A page from the 1924 Paramount catalogue.

affiliate, English Columbia bought a controlling interest in its erstwhile parent.

It may have been this change of management early in 1926 which was responsible for the widening of the Columbia race series. Previously Columbia had done some recording in the field, like

OKeh, mainly of hillbilly material, although just one blues disc in the 14000D series had been recorded outside New York – 14106D by 'Doc' Dasher, made in Atlanta in September 1925. In April 1926 the Columbia field unit made some race recordings in New Orleans and then went on to Atlanta, where they recorded blues singer Virginia Childs, a gospel quartet and a preacher.

Since 1921 OKeh and Paramount had been recording unaccompanied male quartets singing novelty and jazz numbers, which were often issued in the popular series (having a considerable white sale). From the early days of the 12000 race series Paramount had been featuring quartets singing spirituals – the most popular was the Norfolk Jubilee Quartet – and was the only one of the major race companies to make regular issues of this type of music. Now, in Atlanta, Columbia recorded the Birmingham Jubilee Singers. Their first record, *He Took My Sins Away* and *Crying To The Lord* on Columbia 14140D, sold

nearly 5,000 copies and their second more than 13,000; the group recorded prolifically for Columbia, and then for Vocalion, over the next four years. Soon all the companies were looking for gospel quartets – over seventy records of this type of music were issued in 1927 and its popularity has continued to the present day. Except for the lean years of 1932–34 a minimum of thirty gospel quartet records was put out each year until 1941.

But the most important item from Columbia's Atlanta visit was four 'sermons with singing' by a local preacher, Rev J. M. Gates, assisted by two unidentified female members of his congregation. On *Death's Black Train Is Coming*, Rev Gates announces: 'I want to sing a song tonight, and while I sing I want every sinner in the house to come to the angel's feet and bow, and accept prayer – you *need* prayer. Subject of this song, Death's Black Train Is Coming – it's coming, too.' The unaccompanied voices then sing about the hell-bound train, that will bring judgement to all transgressors:

> Some men and some women, they care nothing for the
>   gospel life,
> Till the bell ring and the whistle blows, for the little
>   black train's in sight
> *Refrain:*
> The little black train is coming, get all your business
>   right,
> You better get your house in order, for that train may be
>   here tonight

The singing had a compelling rhythm; the song concerned a metaphor popular amongst black Christians, and the Columbia engineers had arranged for a train whistle to sound several times in the background. When the selection was issued in July 1926 on Columbia 14145D, backed with a slow dirge *Need Of Prayer*, it was an instantaneous success. The previous year Columbia had issued some sermons by Calvin P. Dixon, nicknamed Black Billy Sunday, and Paramount a couple by Rev W. A. White, but the Gates coupling contained the first sermons *with singing*. The advance pressing order for 14145D was 3,675; when the remaining two sides from Gates' Atlanta session were issued in October, on Columbia 14159D, the advance order was 34,025.

As soon as he saw how well Gates' first disc was selling, Polk Brockman – the Atlanta talent scout who had engineered the first

"Waiting at the Beautiful Gate"

Sermon & Singing

by

Rev. J. M. Gates
& Congregation

VOCALION
RECORD
No 1051

There is somebody waiting for everyone up there at that beautiful gate. Maybe it's your own dear mother—or your dear old dad—or your sister—or your brother. Whoever it is, they are there, waiting, waiting for you.

Hear Rev. J. M. Gates, of Atlanta, Ga., tell you who is waiting for him at that beautiful gate. His sermon and his singing is mighty powerful and you'll like every bit of it. On the other side is "Tell Me How You Feel," another great sermon by Rev. Gates.

ASK TO
HEAR

I'm Gonna Shout All Over God's Heaven
We'll Be Ready When the Great Day Comes
Male Quartet with Piano by Perry Bradford   Cotton Belt Quartet   1091

Lord, I've Done What You Told Me To   Male Quartet   1086
Golden Slippers   Piano by Perry Bradford   Cotton Belt Quartet   1/4

Go Down Moses   23688
By an' By   Piano Acc. by Lawrence Brown   Roreland Hayes   75c

BETTER AND CLEANER RACE RECORDS

Vocalion Records

ELECTRICALLY RECORDED
Manufactured by The Brunswick-Balke-Collender Co., Chicago

39

OKeh field trip three years earlier – visited the preacher at his home and signed an exclusive contract with him (Columbia had neglected to do so). Every record company was wanting to issue sermons, preferably sermons by Rev Gates. Brockman took Gates and some members of his congregation up to New York about the beginning of September and had him record for no less than five different record companies – OKeh, Victor, BBC's Vocalion, Pathe and Banner. Gates recorded forty-two sides within the space of two or three weeks and although he did not record any one sermon for all five companies there was plenty of repetition. *The Dying Gambler* was put on wax in the OKeh, Victor and Banner studios, and new versions of *Death's Black Train Is Coming* were made for Victor and Pathé. Gates was recorded again by OKeh when they came to Atlanta in November, and later that month Brockman took him back to New York to make eight sides for Gennett and seven, including yet another version of *Death's Black Train*, for Banner. By this time other preachers were being discovered – OKeh had got hold of Rev H. R. Tomlin (whose first record was *his* version of *Death's Black Train*); Columbia lured Rev J. C. Burnett away from Meritt and discovered Rev W. M. Mosley; Victor recorded Rev Mose Doolittle. In a nine-month period – from September 1926 to June 1927 – sixty records of sermons were put out by the various companies, and no less than forty of them were by Rev J. M. Gates!

Victor recorded Rev Gates in New York and Chicago in 1926 and in Atlanta in 1927. Of the eighteen records issued, eleven were still listed in the 1930 Victor catalogue.

G

GATES, REV. J. M.—Sermons

Rev. Gates

Adam and Eve in Garden			20365
Amazing Grace			20216
Bank That Never Fails			21414
Building That Never Gives Away			21414
Do It Yourself			21523
Dry Bones in the Valley			35810
Dying Mother and Child			20216
First Born			21125
From the Pit to the Throne		V	-38016
Funeral Train			20217
Hebrew Children	20421	Kidnapping	21281
He Was Born in a Manger	21030	Moses in Wilderness	20421
If You Say You Got Religion	V-38016	Samson and the Woman	21125
I Know I Got Religion	20217	Somebody's Been Stealing	21281
Jesus Rose from the Dead	35810	Sure-Enough Soldier	21523
Just As Soon	20365	You May Be Alive	21030

INTO THE FIELD
1927-1930

The years 1927 to 1930 were the peak years of blues recording. There were in 1927 just five hundred blues and gospel records issued, an increase of fifty percent on the already high 1926 figure. This rate of release – an industry average of almost ten new records each week – was steadily maintained until the end of 1930. The companies were able to maintain the flow of music only through exhaustive searches for new talent. Paramount – the market leader during the peak years – brought a wide variety of artists north to its Chicago studios. The other companies made frequent excursions to the major towns in the south: during these four years Atlanta was visited seventeen times by field units in search of race talent, Memphis eleven times, Dallas eight times, New Orleans seven times, and so on. (Full details of all these field trips are included in the authors' comprehensive discography, *Blues and Gospel Records, 1902–1942*.)

During the peak years there were five main companies manufacturing records for the coloured market. General Phonograph had been unable to secure rights to electrical recording and – feeling that they could not, using the old acoustic method, compete effectively with Victor and Columbia – sold their OKeh-Odeon record division to Columbia in October 1926. It was continued as the OKeh Phonograph Corporation, a Columbia subsidiary. For three years after the take-over, the Columbia and OKeh labels were run by quite separate managements, but care was taken that they did not compete for the same artists (Rev Gates' first record were on Columbia, but Columbia was the only label not to record him during the 'sermon boom'; he eventually became an exclusive OKeh artist). And the Columbia 14000D series was enlarged, at the expense of the OKeh 8000s. In 1926 only about fifty blues and gospel records had appeared on Columbia, compared with over a hundred on OKeh. The Columbia releases gradually increased and the OKehs dwindled until in 1929 about eighty-five blues and gospel items were put on the 14000D series as against only around sixty-five in the OKeh 8000 series. OKeh was still a major race label – and it always bore far more good jazz than Columbia – but it was not the power it had been in the classic blues period. The other major race companies during the peak years were Paramount, Brunswick-Balke-Collender with its Vocalion and Brunswick labels, the small Gennett concern, and Victor.

The record industry as a whole had not been in too healthy a state during the early twenties. After the boom year of 1921, in which for the first time 100 million discs were sold, sales declined slowly but steadily. Eventually even Victor began to feel the squeeze – their sales fell from $51 million in 1921 to $44 million in 1923, and then dropped to $20 million in 1925. Something had to be done, and one obvious move was for Victor to begin large-

The 1929 Victor catalogue had an out-of-date minstrel motif on the front cover, and a fairly unrepresentative 'selected list'.

I Shall Not Be Moved Join That Band Taskiana Four	20183
Everybody Got to Walk This Lonesome Valley You Gonna Reap Just What You Sow Pace Jubilee Singers	20310
St. Louis Blues *Pipe Organ* Lenox Avenue Blues Thomas Waller	20357
Someday Sweetheart Blues Original Jelly-Roll Blues Morton's Red Hot Peppers	20405
Kansas City Shuffle Yazoo Blues Moten's Kansas City Orch.	20485
Black Cat Bone Blues *Harmonica, Guitar* Dirty Guitar Blues Bobby Leecan-Robert Cooksey	20251
Savannah Blues *Organ* Won't You Take Me Home?—Fox Trot Waller-Morris' Babies	20776
Stingy Woman—Blues Sun Brimmers—Blues Memphis Jug Band	20552
Jacksonville Blues Them Piano Blues Jacksonville Harmony Trio	20960
Cicero and Cæsar—Part 3 *Comic Dialog* Cicero and Cæsar—Part 4 Jones and Jones	21237
Broken Hearted So Blue Carroll C. Tate	20912
I'm So Glad Today Mother's Prayer A. C. Forehand	20547
Daniel Prayed Three Times a Day Take Me to the Water Rev. E. D. Campbell	20546
Jonah in the Belly of the Whale With His Stripes We Are Healed Rev. McGee	20773

12-inch. List Price $1.25

Dry Bones in the Valley *Sermon* Jesus Rose from the Dead *Sermon* Rev. Gates	35810

scale production of race records, and compete for a market that had been growing at an enormous rate during the period when overall sales had been falling. In July 1926 – almost three years since the last race session in a Victor studio – blues singers Mike Jackson and Mabel Richardson were recorded. Victor's first efforts were not too promising – they included Elizabeth Smith, a minor singer in the classic style, a gospel quartet called the Taskiana Four, Mamie Smith (who had been dropped by OKeh at the end of 1923 and then briefly featured on Ajax in '24) and the inevitable sermons by Rev Gates. There was little else they could do – the best artists were under contract to Paramount, OKeh or Columbia.

Then Victor hired Ralph Peer, who had been largely responsible for building up OKeh's fine race and hillbilly catalogues. Peer realised that Victor was several years too late to be able to get a substantial share of the classic blues market and decided to concentrate his efforts on the country blues field. In February 1927 Peer set out with the Victor field unit, calling first at Atlanta where he recorded thirty titles by white hillbilly performers and four selections by country blues singer Julius Daniels. After six days in Atlanta the unit moved on to Memphis where, between 24th February and 1st March, they recorded thirty titles by black jazz bands, preachers, guitar evangelists and blues singers. Peer had visited Memphis ahead of the field unit and – on the recommendation of Charlie Williamson, black bandleader and talent scout – had auditioned the Memphis Jug Band, a group consisting of a kazoo-player, a jug-blower and two guitarists, one of whom doubled on harmonica. Peer thought the group had market potential and they were the first artists recorded, on the morning of Thursday, 24th February, in the temporary studio set up in the McCall building.

The final call was New Orleans, and Victor again concentrated on black performers – including Louis Dumaine's Jazzola Eight, Rev Isaiah Shelton and Richard 'Rabbit' Brown, a guitar-picking ferryboat man, who recorded *James Alley Blues* and *I'm Not Jealous* (on Victor 20578) as well as two long ballads *The Mystery Of Dunbar's Child* and *The Sinking Of The Titanic* (issued on a 12-inch disc, 35840). Of the blues recorded on this tour the big successes were the titles by the Memphis Jug Band. *Sun Brimmer's Blues* and *Stingy Woman Blues*, on 20552 in the general series, sold so well that Peer asked leader Will Shade to bring the group to Chicago to record four more titles, on Thursday, 9th June.

Mayo Williams' label was named after concert artist Sissieretta Jones – nicknamed 'The Black Patti', she was perhaps the best known of all black singers.

Early in 1927 Mayo Williams, who had done so much to build up the Paramount race list, resigned in order to start his own Chicago Record Company. In May the *Chicago Defender* carried the first advertisement for Williams' Black Patti records. All the titles had been recorded for Williams by Gennett, and at least half the material was also issued on Gennett's own labels. Black Patti featured jazz bands, choirs, some fine blues singers (including Sam Collins from Mississippi) and – despite the label name – two white crooners. Black Patti adverts appeared in thirteen successive weekly editions of the *Defender* and then suddenly stopped; the last issue was *You Heard Me Whistle* and *Boll Weavil* by harmonica-playing Jaybird Coleman, on Black Patti 8055.

Meanwhile, Brunswick-Balke-Collender were still struggling to establish their Vocalion race series. Spurred by the success of records by unaccompanied gospel quartets, and sermons in the Rev Gates style, BBC pioneered a third type of religious record – gospel songs by itinerant guitar-playing evangelists. In November 1926 they recorded Blind Joe Taggart performing numbers like

REV.
A. W. NIX

REV. E. W.
CLAYBORN

JOE
TAGGART

From a Vocalion sleeve, late 1927 or early 1928.

45

Take Your Burden To The Lord and *Just Beyond Jordan* (issued on Vocalion 1061) and in December Edward W. Clayborn, a powerful singer who played a singing bottle-neck guitar, made *The Gospel Train Is Coming* and *Your Enemy Cannot Harm You (But Watch Your Close Friend)*. When these titles were first issued, on Vocalion 1082, the artist credit was just 'The Guitar Evangelist'; however the record sold so well that it was re-pressed many times during the next few years and the label seems to have been printed afresh each time – copies have been found labelled Edward W. Clayburn, Edward W. Clayborn and even Rev Edward W. Clayton! Religious singers like Taggart and Clayborn sang in the same general style and led the same sort of life as country blues singers like Blind Lemon Jefferson; they were distinguished only by their choice of material. Taggart in fact recorded one secular number – *C & O Blues* on Vocalion 1116 – making sure that this appeared under the pseudonym of Blind Amos.

But, successful as were their religious issues, BBC were not doing at all well on the blues side. They needed someone to search out likely talent. When Mayo Williams' Black Patti venture folded in August 1927, Vocalion had no hesitation in hiring him as talent scout for the 1000 series. In October, Mayo Williams brought an old medicine show entertainer called Jim Jackson to BBC's Chicago headquarters and recorded six minutes of *Jim Jackson's Kansas City Blues*:

> I woke up this morning feeling bad
> Thought about the good times I once have had
> *Refrain:*
> I'm gonna move to Kansas City, I'm gonna move to
>   Kansas City
> I'm gonna move baby, honey where they don't like you

It was released, on the two sides of Vocalion 1144, on 8th December 1927 and was an immediate hit. Vocalion had found an artist whose appeal matched that of Victor's Memphis Jug Band. Jim Jackson was called back to Chicago in January to record eight more selections, including Parts 3 and 4 of *Jim Jackson's Kansas City Blues*.

The cover of Victor's 1930 catalogue, without the legend 'Race Records', prominent in 1929, and with a more appropriate picture.

The first country blues singer to appear on the Columbia 14000D series was Peg Leg Howell, recorded in Atlanta in November 1926 and again the following April. Atlanta was a centre for white folk music and – like all other record companies – Columbia went there mainly for hillbilly talent; but they also kept a lookout for good country blues singers. The field unit was in Atlanta from 25th March to 8th April 1927 and although only

about thirty of the 200 titles recorded were by black artists, they included two tunes by Robert Hicks, a versatile singer who accompanied himself on the 12-string guitar. *Barbecue Blues* and *Cloudy Sky Blues* were put out under the name Barbecue Bob on Columbia 14205D; 10,850 copies were pressed and the record issued on May 10th. Initial sales were so good that Hicks was called to New York in the middle of June to record eight more numbers. And when Columbia returned to Atlanta in November they recorded not only a further eight selections by Barbecue Bob, but also six by his brother Charley Lincoln, who sang the same sort of songs in very much the same style.

In December 1927 Frank Walker took the Columbia field unit to Dallas and Memphis. Nearly all the time in Dallas was devoted to race artists – three or four blues singers and two popular gospel singers, Washington Phillips, who accompanied himself on the dulceola, an unusual instrument of the dulcimer family, and Blind Willie Johnson, a singer with an incredibly rough, powerful voice that was perfectly complemented by his virtuoso guitar. In Memphis, Columbia recorded a couple of preachers and two blues singers, Reubin Lacy from Mississippi and Lewis Black from Arkansas. They issued a record by Lewis Black in March 1928 but it must have sold badly for Black's other two sides were not released until June 1929; none of the Lacy titles were issued. Columbia did not return to Memphis.

Since late 1925, OKeh had been issuing a new record every six weeks by singer-guitarist Lonnie Johnson. Johnson was not exactly a country blues singer – he had visited London in a musical revue from 1917 to 1919, and worked as a jazz-band vocalist – but his material and style were on the outer edge of the country blues idiom. After the take-over by Columbia, OKeh made no field trips for a while. Then, in February 1928, they visited Memphis to record a number of hillbilly and race artists some of whom (like Rev Gates) had travelled west from Georgia and others (such as blues singers Tom Dickson and John Hurt) had come north from Mississippi. Lonnie Johnson went with the unit, himself recording in both Memphis and San Antonio. In San Antonio he also provided the guitar accompaniment for Texas Alexander, a shouting rural singer who had been recorded in New York by OKeh the previous August.

Columbia illustrated the polite face of Billy Bird's double-entendre; Mill Man Blues *was recorded in Atlanta on 29th October 1928.*

"Magic Notes"

"Mill Man Blues"

"Now, lady, I ain't no mill man
Just the mill man's son
But I can do your grinding
Till the mill man comes"

And how he does the grinding is well told on this rollicking Columbia Record, with "Down in the Cemetery," another mean blues number, on the other side.

The pattern was now set for the next few years. Columbia visited Atlanta each spring and autumn to replenish the hillbilly catalogue, and also made a few race recordings; the late autumn of each year they went to Dallas, to make further titles by Blind Willie Johnson and Washington Phillips, and some by the accomplished Texas pianist-singers—men like Whistlin' Alex Moore and Texas Bill Day. OKeh paid regular visits to Atlanta and San Antonio for hillbilly material, and usually recorded a few black artists at each location. Victor went to Atlanta once or twice a year for hillbilly material, and also recorded a few titles for the race catalogue (generally including four new numbers by the Atlanta blues singer and twelve-string guitarist Blind Willie McTell, who also contrived to be recorded by Columbia under the pseudonym Blind Sammie).

Victor was the only company systematically to exploit the gold mine of black talent in and around Memphis. Their second visit there, in January and February 1928, yielded three times as much material as the initial visit in early '27 – and again black artists greatly outnumbered white hillbilly performers. Besides more titles by the Memphis Jug Band, Victor recorded the Cannon's Jug Stompers, Vocalion's popular artist Jim Jackson, and a fine group of Mississippi blues singers – Tommy Johnson, Ishman Bracey and Frank Stokes. Stokes was an oldish man, his voice had a pronounced vibrato and his style of singing and guitar playing were distinctly archaic. His *Downtown Blues* and *Bedtime Blues* on Victor 21272 sold well and when Victor returned to Memphis in August 1928 they recorded ten further selections by Stokes.

The August visit was Victor's most extensive to date. Between Monday 27th August and Monday 24th September they recorded 180 titles, three-quarters of them by race artists. They would normally record between six and eight tunes each day (the most they ever managed in a day was twelve), recording two takes of each item, or three if there had been something amiss with either of the first two. All the singers they had tried out in February were recorded again, and new ones besides. Jim Jackson recorded twelve more items, including a two-part *I'm Gonna Move To Louisiana*, that had the same tune and almost the same words as his *Kansas City Blues*. The autumn trip to Memphis now became an annual event for Victor – it was here that they recorded most of their race material.

Although Vocalion had become a major producer of race records at about the same time as Victor, they were slower to take recording equipment into the field. Then in 1928 they recorded some not too exciting blues artists in Dallas, New Orleans and Atlanta, and several gospel performers in Birmingham, Alabama; although they did stop at Memphis, only two race titles were recorded, fairly dull tunes by a singer who styled himself 'Keghouse'. Not until 1929 did they do any significant recording in the south.

It is difficult to know whether it was by luck or guile that the Vocalion field unit arrived in Memphis – in mid-September 1929 – just about a week before Victor was due. The Memphis Jug Band and Cannon's Jug Stompers were under contract to Victor, and Vocalion could not use them; but they did manage to snatch a number of worthwhile performers from under Victor's nose, including blues singer Robert Wilkins (whom Victor had recorded the previous autumn) and Speckled Red, whose raucous piano number *The Dirty Dozens* became one of Brunswick-Balke-Collender's most successful releases.

During the peak years there were fewer small companies producing

By 1930 Frank Stokes had been featured on seven Victor race records; Tain't Nobody's Business was on both sides of V-38500.

Stevedore Stomp—Fox Trot *The Dicty Glide—Fox Trot*	Ellington's Cotton Club Orchestra *Ellington's Cotton Club Orchestra*	**V-** 38053	10	.75
Stingy Woman—Blues *Sun Brimmers—Blues*	Memphis Jug Band *Memphis Jug Band*	20532	10	.75
St. James Infirmary *with Vocal Refrain* *When You're Smiling—Fox Trot*	King Oliver and His Orch. *King Oliver and His Orchestra*	22298	10	.75
St. Louis Blues *After You've Gone* *Piano Duet*	"Fats" Waller-Bennie Paine *"Fats" Waller-Bennie Paine*	22371	10	.75
St. Louis Blues *I'm a Broken-Hearted Blackbird*	Leroy Smith and His Orchestra *Leroy Smith and His Orchestra*	21472	10	.75
St. Louis Blues *Pipe Organ* *Lenox Avenue Blues*	 Thomas Waller *Thomas Waller*	20357	10	.75

Frank Stokes

STOKES, FRANK—with Guitar

Bedtime Blues	21272
Bunker Hill Blues	V-38548
Downtown Blues	21272
How Long?	V-38512
I Got Mine	V-38512
It Won't Be Long Now	21672
Mistreatin' Blues	21672
Nehi Mamma Blues	21738
South Memphis Blues	V-38548
Stomp That Thing	21738
'Taint' Nobody's Business	V-38500
Take Me Back	V-38531
What's the Matter Blues	V-38531

Stompin' On Down—Fox Trot *Tiny's Stomp—Fox Trot*	"Tiny" Parham and His Musicians *"Tiny" Parham and His Musicians*	**V-** 38060	10	.75
Stomp That Thing *Nehi Mamma Blues* *with Guitar*	Frank Stokes *Frank Stokes*	21738	10	.75
Stop Dat Band *Creep Along Moses*	Taskiana Four *Taskiana Four*	20184	10	.75

just half-a-dozen or so race records each year. They either dropped out of the market altogether, or increased their output, like Vocalion and Gennett. In 1926 Pathé decided to compete more seriously for this expanding market and announced a race series on their Perfect label. Perfect 101 and 102 – by Rosa Henderson, under the pseudonym Mamie Harris, and Mary Stafford, the singer Columbia had dropped at the end of 1921 – were released in July 1926. In a period when the market was crying out for country blues, Perfect put out second-rate selections by minor classic blues singers, like Rosa Henderson, seasoned with a few sermons by Rev Gates. Although Perfect records sold for only 39 cents, the public evidently preferred to pay 75 cents for the more up-to-the-minute material on Paramount, Victor, OKeh, Columbia or Vocalion. The Perfect race series had reached number 136 by the end of 1927; only two or three more records appeared on it in the next three years.

Left: a Vocalion sleeve from late 1929. Gennett printed 'Race Record' on the label, and showed the month of issue. Riverside Blues was recorded about 23rd April 1927, issued in August 1927, and withdrawn from the catalogue on 30th January 1930.

January 1927 saw the emergence of Gennett as a major race label. Of all the major producers it was the only one never to have a separate race series; yet strangely enough it was the only company to print the words 'Race Record' on the record label (and had been doing so since late in 1924). Gennett's first electric recording had appeared in 1926, on the 50-cent 3000 series. However, the high royalty which had to be paid for the privilege of using electric recording techniques made a price increase necessary; a new 6000 'Electrobeam' general series was started in '27, selling at 75 cents. Some first-class blues artists appeared in this series, including the honkytonk pianist Cow Cow Davenport and Cryin' Sam Collins, the earliest of the great Mississippi blues singers to record.

Nevertheless, the volume of sales continued to be poor, and Gennett only managed to keep their heads above water by paying low artist fees. For example, in 1925 Baby Bonnie was paid $15 per title for *Longing Blues* and *Home Sweet Home Blues* on Gennett 3041, the pianist $10 and the trumpeter $5. And the same year singer John Henry Howard was paid $30 for nine titles! After 1925 royalties were offered rather than a flat fee – average payment was one cent less 10% per side sold.

Although talent scouts were regularly employed, only one field trip was made: to Birmingham, Alabama, where a temporary studio was rigged up in the local Starr Music Store (probably the reason Birmingham was chosen). Recording lasted from July to the end of August 1927 and included a preacher, a quartet, harmonica-player Jaybird Coleman (on no less than eighteen titles) and a number of blues singers. Only one of the two titles recorded in Birmingham by William Harris was issued, on Gennett 6306; but Harris's high-pitched voice, competent guitar and his original treatment of traditional material must have sold for he was called to Gennett's headquarters in Richmond, Indiana, in October 1928 to record fourteen more numbers.

In order to compete with cheap labels such as Pathé's Perfect, in September 1925 Gennett initiated the Champion label, at 35 cents each or three for $1. Almost everything that appeared on Gennett was also put out on Champion. Later they also issued some blues material on the cheap Superior label, selling exclusively through chain stores. In addition, the mail-order firm of Sears Roebuck put out Gennett race items on its established cut-price label Silvertone and also, from 1928, on Supertone. All issues on these cheap labels were under pseudonym, in order to hide the fact that identical material was being issued on Gennett for 75 cents and on the other labels for less than half the price. Thus Lottie Kimbrough – a massive singer who was billed as Lottie Beaman, 'The Kansas City Butter Ball' by Paramount – appeared under her own name on Gennett, as Lottie Everson on Champion, as Lottie Brown on Supertone, and as Martha Johnson on Superior. Sam Collins was labelled Jim Foster on Champion and Silvertone.

In December 1925 a most interesting label made its appearance. Called Herwin, and produced by *Her*bert and Ed*win* Schiele of the St Louis Music Company, it was sold mainly through advertisements in farm journals, for 75 cents, an exceptionally high price for mail-order records. Three companies – two of whom were Gennett and Paramount – were known to have pressed, labelled and shipped these records for Herwin, which accounts for the same issue number being used twice, for quite different couplings, in some instances. To save costs, the quality of material used for pressing was very poor and the records wore out quickly. Owing to these factors sales were bad and in 1930 Herwin was sold to Paramount after seventy-three issues – almost all pseudonymous – over four years.

The only race company that made no field trips whatever during the peak years was Paramount. Yet, both in number of records released, and in the range of singers recorded, Paramount was the market leader. During each of the peak years Paramount issued more than one hundred blues and gospel records (in addition

'The Georgia Sacred Singers' concealed the identity of the Norfolk Jubilee Quartet; this title was also issued on Paramount 12630.

to a fair amount of jazz and some novelty numbers). Gennett issued around forty each year; Columbia altogether 150 in their two established series – OKeh 8000 and Columbia 14000D. And although the Victor race catalogue was of a high quality, the quantity was not great – about sixty a year. The main emphasis in the peak years was on the country blues, but the best of the classic singers still sold well; Sara Martin and Sippie Wallace were dropped by OKeh at the end of 1927, but Bessie Smith, Ma Rainey, Victoria Spivey and Clara Smith continued to have a new record issued about every other month.

The great gospel boom had been in late 1926; Rev J. C. Burnett's first record on Columbia – *Downfall Of Nebuchadnezzar* and *I've Even Heard Of Thee*, exactly the same titles as on his earlier Meritt release – sold 80,000 copies soon after its release in November '26; this was four times as many as the normal sale of a Bessie Smith record, and Bessie was still outselling just about every other blues singer. But the bubble soon burst and Burnett's fourth record, in March '27, had initial sales in the region of 15,000. However this was still rather more than for the average blues record, and sermons continued to be a worthwhile proposition throughout the peak years. Besides Gates and Burnett, two Chicago preachers were well represented in the catalogues. Victor had secured Rev F. W. McGee, who accompanied himself on the piano and often included a cornet, guitar and drums as well – his records had a swinging, jazzy flavour. Vocalion had Rev A. W. Nix, whose *Black Diamond Express To Hell* was perhaps the best known

Rev. F. W. McGee was Victor's most successful preacher.

Mary Lee—Fox Trot	Bennie Moten's Kansas City Orchestra	V–		
Sweetheart of Yesterday—Fox Trot	*Bennie Moten's Kansas City Orch.*	38114	10	.75

McGEE, REV. F. W.—Sermons

Babylon Is Falling Down		21090
City of Pure Gold	V	-38005
Crooked Made Straight		21090
Crucifixion of Jesus	V	-38028
Dead Cat on the Line	V	-38579
Death May Be Your		21656
From the Jailhouse	V	-38528
Half Ain't Never Been Told		21492
He Is a Saviour for Me		20858
He's Got the World	V	-38513
Holes in Your Pockets	V	-38583
Holy City		21205
I Looked Down the Line	V	-38561
I've Seen the Devil	V	-38583
Jesus Cried	V	-38536
Jesus in the Fire	V	-38574
Jesus, the Light	V	-38513
Jesus the Lord	V	-38561
Jonah in the Whale		20773
Love of God	V	-38005

Rev. F. W. McGee

sermon of any period: Parts 1 and 2 appeared on Vocalion 1098 in May '27, Parts 3 and 4 on Vocalion 1421, released in November 1929, and Parts 5 and 6 on Vocalion 1486, in June 1930. The theme was basically the same as that of the record that started it all – *Death's Black Train Is Coming* by Rev J. M. Gates. The Vocalion advert announced 'Here she comes! The *"Black Diamond Express To Hell"* with Sin, the Engineer, holding the throttle wide open; Pleasure is the Headlight, and the Devil is the Conductor. You can feel the roaring of the Express and the moanin' of the Drunkards, Liars, Gamblers and other folk who have got aboard. They are hell-bound and they don't want to go. The train makes eleven stops but nobody can get off . . .'; and they appended a map of the express's route, marking the stops: 'Liars' Ave', 'Dance Hall Depot', 'Stealing Town', and so on.

In 1927 one third of the 500 releases were gospel items; the figure dropped to about a quarter in 1928 and remained at this level for the next two years. There was an annual output of around fifty sermons, fifty records by unaccompanied quartets, and twenty or so by guitar evangelists. Besides the regular evangelists – Blind Joe Taggart, Blind Willie Johnson, Edward W. Clayborn and Paramount's Blind Willie Davis – quite a few blues singers tried their hand at gospel numbers, the records often being issued under a pseudonym. Thus Barbecue Bob assumed his real name – Robert Hicks – for religious numbers, and the two gospel issues from Blind Lemon Jefferson were labelled 'Deacon L. J. Bates', the L. J. being a rather obvious clue.

Paramount issued almost twice as many blues and gospel items in 1927 as they had in 1926. Their best-selling artists were recorded at a tremendous rate, reminiscent of the overissuing of classic blues singers in '23 and '24. New Blind Lemon and Blind Blake discs appeared just about every month. (Victor, in contrast, were considerably more cautious – even Memphis Jug Band releases were held at six a year.) So successful was Blind Lemon that a special yellow and white label was produced for Paramount 12650 *Piney Woods Money Mama* and *Low Down Mojo Blues*, bearing his picture and the legend 'Blind Lemon Jefferson's Birthday Record.'

Paramount's New York studio having closed down in 1926, artists continued to record in Chicago until, in 1929, new studios were opened in Grafton, Wisconsin; by the end of the year all recordings were made here. This was the era of the very best in blues and gospel recording. Paramount had issued material by

Frank Stokes and his partner Dan Sane, under the name Beale Street Sheiks, and by Gus Cannon, under the name Banjo Joe, in 1927, before Victor signed them. Full credit must go to the talent scouts, foremost of whom was Henry C. Spiers, a music-store owner from Jackson, Mississippi, who searched the south for talent to send up to the Paramount studios. Among the artists Spiers unearthed were Son House, who had an unforgettable ringing guitar style, Skip James, an original singer who transferred his guitar technique wholesale to the piano, and the great Charley Patton. Paramount asked Gennett to record fourteen tunes by Patton at their Richmond, Indiana studio in June 1929; the first issue was *Pony Blues* and *Banty Rooster Blues*, on Paramount 12792. Patton was a light-skinned man with curly blond hair, but his appearance was deceptive. Patton's deep rough voice blurred over the lyrics and often descended into incomprehensibility – it was perfectly complemented by his clear-toned fluent guitar; as with Blind Lemon, the guitar often took over the vocal line. Patton's whole performance produced a riveting, hypnotic effect, perhaps comparable to that of an African witch-doctor.

Realising that they had a star in Patton, Paramount labelled his second blues release – *Screamin' And Hollerin' Blues* on Paramount 12805 in September 1929 – 'The Masked Marvel'. The advert bore a drawing of a blindfolded singer – looking nothing like Patton – and the clue that this was an exclusive Paramount artist. Anyone correctly guessing the Masked Marvel's identity would get a free Paramount record of their choice. There must have been many records claimed, for no one else could be mistaken for Patton. Eager to exploit all angles, Paramount also put out two gospel items by Patton under the pseudonym Elder J. J. Hadley. In 1930 he had thirteen records issued – more than any other blues artist.

Paramount also had a number of cheap, three-for-a-dollar, subsidiary labels. One of these, Broadway, featured a race series – pseudonymously as usual, to disguise the fact that it merely duplicated material from the higher-priced label. Ma Rainey appeared on Broadway as Lila Patterson, Ida Cox as Kate Lewis and as Velma Bradley; Blind Lemon, however, was issued on Broadway without a pseudonym.

In January 1928 Paramount's recording manager, Arthur E. Satherley, left to work for QRS records (no one has yet discovered what – if anything – these initials stand for), taking with him those masters to which he had personal rights. Most of these items, already issued on Paramount in many cases, appeared in the QRS 7000 race series, but the series mainly consisted of material recorded by QRS at Long Island City – including ten titles by Clifford Gibson, a mellow singer from Louisville who was afterwards signed by Victor. However, QRS soon lost interest in the 7000 series and it was discontinued after number 7092, in 1929.

1927 had been a glorious year for all types of recording, with industry sales exceeding 100 million for the first time since 1921. Victor's receipts had climbed back to $48 million, more than double what they had been in 1925. Exact figures are not available,

James (Stump) Johnson was recorded by QRS at Long Island City about January 1929; this was one of a batch of QRS masters re-issued on Paramount towards the end of 1929, after QRS had decided to abandon race recording.

but it seems probable that race records were making up 5%, or a little more, of total industry sales. The average blues or gospel record had sales in the region of ten thousand. In 1928 the figure was a thousand or so lower; but it was still a thriving market and the future looked rosy. In January 1929 Victor decided to inaugurate a special race series (race releases had until then been mingled into the general series). The V38000 series at first contained both jazz and vocal issues, but after V38035 it was decided to reserve it for instrumental performances, and the V38500 series – begun in April '29 – carried the blues and gospel items.

Benefiting from Mayo Williams's know-how, Vocalion were steadily increasing their share of the market. Their three releases a month in 1926 gave way to four the next year and five in 1928. Brunswick-Balke-Collender started a second race series, the Brunswick 7000s, in May 1927 but only issued a handful of miscellaneous records on it in the following eighteen months. Then, in 1929, BBC issued around ninety blues and gospel records in the Vocalion 1000 series and also put out fifty in the Brunswick race series; these figures were repeated the following year. The sudden expansion was made possible partly through intensive recording activity in the field, and partly through Mayo Williams's discovery of three new and extraordinarily popular artists.

In June 1928 Vocalion took a unit to Indianapolis to record Leroy Carr, an urban singer who accompanied himself on the piano – a welcome contrast to the rural singer-guitarists who could now be heard by the dozen on all the major labels. The lead side on Carr's first record – released on Vocalion 1191, in mid-August '28 – was *How Long How Long Blues*, a lament for a girl friend who had travelled away up the railroad:

> How long, how long, has that evening train been gone
> How long, how long, baby how long

The tune was as unforgettable as Jim Jackson's *Kansas City Blues* of the year before. Carr's full, mournful singing, and the brilliance of his piano and the guitar of his partner Scrapper Blackwell combined to make a runaway hit. He was called to Chicago to record six more tunes in August, and in December he returned to make *How Long How Long Blues* Parts 2 and 3 (on Vocalion 1241 and 1279 respectively). Vocalion issued ten records by Carr in 1929, and the same number the following year.

Mississippi singer Ishman Bracey recorded for Victor in 1928, and then for Paramount in 1930.

In May 1928 Vocalion finally dropped their tag 'Better and Cleaner Race Records'. This was an honest thing to do, since their releases had been as full of innuendo as anyone else's. But it also showed considerable foresight, for the artists Mayo Williams brought to the studio in September that year specialised in the most suggestive lyrics in the business. Hudson Whittaker, otherwise known as Tampa Red 'The Guitar Wizard', and pianist Georgia Tom Dorsey recorded *It's Tight Like That*, released on Vocalion 1216. The gradually accelerating tempo, Tampa Red's open bottle-neck guitar playing and the sly humour with which the simple lyrics were delivered produced an irresistibly erotic effect. Soon the record was being played and copied everywhere. Tampa Red was in such demand that in 1929 he had

Left: Leroy Carr was the first really successful blues pianist, and had a profound influence on many singers of the thirties. Right: Tampa Red's Vocalion records continued to be heavily featured after the label was bought by Warner Brothers, in 1930.

seventeen new records issued, all on Vocalion (numerically, his nearest rivals were Blind Blake and Leroy Carr, with ten apiece, and Blind Lemon Jefferson and Lonnie Johnson, who had nine each).

Victor and Columbia continued to concentrate on their country blues artists, and gave no signs of noticing that a new urban style was sweeping Chicago. But Paramount, as always, lost no time in exploiting the new craze. They created a group called 'The Hokum Boys' (first recorded in December 1928, only a week or two after *It's Tight Like That* was released) that had a variable personnel and specialised in Tampa Red-type numbers – tunes like *Beedle Um Bum*, *Somebody's Been Using That Thing* and *It's All Worn Out*.

In February 1930 the OKeh field unit called at Shreveport, Louisiana, to do some recording at the request of the local radio station. While there, they also recorded a white singer called Blind Andy and a small black group who called themselves the Mississippi Sheiks. The Sheiks sang – often as vocal duets – catchy numbers like *Lonely One In This Town* and *Bootleggers Blues*, and accompanied themselves on a violin and one or two guitars. Their records went down so well that OKeh recorded fourteen more numbers at San Antonio in August and a further sixteen in Jackson, Mississippi, just before Christmas. The Sheiks – with their vaguely hillbilly sound – were producing, within a rural idiom, the same type of music that Tampa Red and Georgia Tom had perfected in Chicago; it was probably no coincidence that one of the selections recorded in San Antonio was *Loose Like That*, issued on OKeh 8820. Their most popular title was *Sitting On Top Of The World* – words heavy with irony, sung at slow tempo against a mournful mocking violin accompaniment:

Was all the summer, and all the fall
Just trying to find my little all and all
Refrain:
But now she's gone, I don't worry
I'm sitting on top of the world

HARD TIMES
1931-1934

At the end of 1930 the record companies were anything but sitting on top of the world. Columbia, for instance, had pressed an average of 11,000 copies of each new blues and gospel record in 1927; in the latter half of 1928 the figure was down to 7,000, and by the end of 1929 it had fallen to 5,000. By May 1930 – in the wake of the Stock Market crash – the company was pressing an average of 2,000, and that figure was halved by the end of the year. As 1931 dawned, race records were selling about a tenth as well as they had four years previously. And the situation continued steadily to worsen. 350 or 400 copies were pressed of each of the last twenty-two discs in the Columbia 14000D series, issued between May and October 1932, and Columbia – still pricing the records at 75 cents – couldn't even sell this small number; all twenty-two were still in catalogue in November 1934.

Paramount was the first company to succumb; their last advertisement in the *Chicago Defender* had been on 26th April 1930 (for 12917, *Mississippi Blues* and *Got To Have My Sweetbread*, by piano bluesman Charlie Spand). Over a hundred blues and gospel items were issued in 1930 but in 1931 the number was down to about three dozen. In 1932 they brought the popular Mississippi Sheiks to Grafton, Wisconsin to record twelve titles (including one called *The New Sittin' On Top Of The World*). The Sheiks sang and played as they never had before but even they could not save Paramount from financial ruin; the last record in the 12000 series – which altogether bore more issues than any other race series – was *She's Crazy 'Bout Her Lovin'* and *Tell Her To Do Right* by the Sheiks, issued on Paramount 13156 in late 1932.

At the end of 1930 the Starr Piano Company discontinued their 75 cent Gennett label but continued to issue some race titles on the cheap Champion and Superior, including records by Scrapper Blackwell, Leroy Carr's guitarist, and by Georgia Tom, Tampa Red's partner (Carr and Tampa Red were both firmly under contract to Vocalion). The Superior label was discontinued in July 1932; the following month a few sides were recorded by members of the Memphis Jug Band but after that recording virtually ceased. In 1933 only seven race titles were recorded – four piano solos by Turner Parrish in January, and three blues with guitar accompaniment by Archie Lewis, in March. Champion still managed to release about a dozen blues discs in 1933, half what they had put out in each of the two previous years, by using rejected titles from earlier years. They continued in this way into 1934 and then, in August, made some new race recordings – four blues by Frank James, accompanying himself on the piano. James was promised a ½-cent royalty per side sold, but just nineteen copies of Champion 16809 – *Snake Hip Blues* backed with *Frank's Lonesome Blues* – had been shipped out of the factory when the company went into liquidation at the end of 1934. It is doubtful if James ever received the nineteen cents he was due.

After its take-over of OKeh, the Columbia company had continued to run the two labels quite independently, with each having its own studio and field unit. In the autumn of 1929 – with sales running at half the 1927 level – they effected some degree of rationalisation and used a single field unit to cover both labels. But the Columbia and OKeh catalogues were still kept as separate as possible. The joint unit went in late '29 to the old OKeh stomping ground of San Antonio, where it recorded just for OKeh issue; then it went to Dallas, Columbia's regular centre, where all recordings were earmarked for Columbia issue. The third stop was New Orleans: Columbia artists – including Blind Willie Johnson – were recorded on 10th and 11th December, and then OKeh artists – amongst them Rev Gates, called down from Atlanta – from 13th until 17th December.

Blind Willie Johnson's first records had sold no better than the average disc in the Columbia 14000D series – in early 1929 they would manage about 5,000 as against Barbecue Bob's 6,000 and Bessie Smith's 9,000 or 10,000. But in mid-1930 the blind evangelist became the star of the list – his records were *still* selling 5,000 copies, although Barbecue Bob was down to 2,000, Bessie Smith to 3,000, and the average release had initial sales of only just over 1,000. Columbia issued seven records by Blind Willie in 1930, but, as times became harder the following year, even his appeal waned. In 1931, like Barbecue Bob, Bessie Smith and the rest, Blind Willie's records were selling in hundreds rather than thousands.

The Columbia label had no new artists, and its releases were cut by over a third in 1931. OKeh was in a slightly better way. They not only had the fast-selling Mississippi Sheiks, but had also been issuing solo records by Bo Carter, a guitar-playing member of the group. Carter gave perfectly straight country blues renditions of songs with simple, risqué lyrics – *Ants In My Pants*, *Same Thing The Cats Fight About* and *Ram Rod Daddy*. His first records went so well that late in 1931 OKeh put out a special batch of three Bo Carters – numbers 8887 to 8889 in the race series. Thanks to the Sheiks and Bo Carter, OKeh managed to issue marginally more blues and gospel than they had the previous year.

But times *were* getting harder. Columbia-OKeh made one field trip in 1931, to Atlanta in October/November. This time the principle of keeping the labels separate was forgotten. The first day they recorded two tunes by Blind Willie McTell which were marked in the ledger 'Blind Sammie' and allocated matrix numbers from the Columbia series; then McTell was recorded singing two more tunes, but this time the name 'Georgia Bill' was entered and the selections given OKeh matrix numbers. A month or two later Blind Willie appeared – under the two different pseudonyms – on Columbia 14632D and OKeh 8936.

That was the last field trip Columbia made. In December 1931 English Columbia sold the American company to Grigsby-Grunow, which had grown fat on the profits of its Majestic radio sets and was seeking to diversify. The new management decided at first to concentrate on Columbia – to the exclusion of OKeh – and continued to release two new items each fortnight in the 14000D series for most of 1932. Bo Carter and Mississippi Sheiks items – originally earmarked for OKeh issue – appeared on Columbia 14671D and 14672D. Then in October they decided that sales did not justify any more releases; 681 discs had appeared in the series, over a period of nine years. The last glimpse of the 14000Ds is in the November 1934 Columbia catalogue, which still lists a few choice items – four by Barbecue Bob, ten by Blind Willie Johnson, fifteen by Bessie Smith (out of the sixty-six discs she had had issued in the 14000Ds) and just one – out of a grand total of fifty-three issued – by Clara Smith. Grigsby-Grunow continued with the OKeh 8000s, issuing a couple of records every other month. They did just a little recording in 1932. four tunes by Clara Smith twelve by Lonnie Johnson and – surprisingly – two by Lucille Hegamin, her first for six years. In 1933 they recorded the Mississippi Sheiks and, after a two-year absence from the studio, Bessie Smith. But this was not because they imagined Bessie would still sell well among her own people – the session was organised at the request of English Parlophone, who were building up a jazz catalogue.

In 1930, when most companies were considering cutting back on their race issues, the American Record Corporation entered the field. ARC had been formed in August 1929 by the merger of three small companies: the Cameo Record Corporation, with labels Cameo and Romeo, the Plaza Music Company, whose labels included Banner and Oriole, and the Pathé Phonograph and Radio Corporation, owners of Perfect. These were all cheap labels, selling at prices much below the regular 75 cents charged by the big companies. Perfect – the most popular of the bunch – had been 39 cents but was reduced to 25 cents at about the time ARC was formed.

The depression, with the massive unemployment it brought, had a shattering effect on the pockets of black record buyers. Race records probably accounted for only about one percent of total industry sales in 1931, as against around five percent four years earlier. There was a clear opening for cut-price race discs. In 1930 ARC decided to revive the Perfect race series, and this time they made sure that they used currently popular artists singing up-to-the-minute material. In April 1930 ARC recorded some solo blues by Georgia Tom, and some Tampa Red-type numbers by

The 1934 Columbia catalogue listed records by Bessie Smith from as far back as 1925; the Clara Smith item was from 1929.

SMITH, BESSIE—Vocal

14663-D Shipwreck Blues / Long Old Road	14354-D Devil's Gonna Git You / Yes Indeed He Do	14129-D What's the Matter Now? / I Want Ev'ry Bit of It
14527-D Blue Spirit Blues / Worn Out Papa Blues	14324-D Spider Man Blues / Put It Right Here	14083-D Careless Love Blues / He's Gone Blues
14451-D Take It Right Back / Nobody Knows You When You're Down	14312-D Empty Bed Blues— in 2 parts	14079-D Dixie Flyer Blues / You've Been a Good Ole Wagon
14427-D I'm Wild About That Thing / You've Got to Give Me Some	14292-D I Used to Be Your Sweet Mamma / Thinking Blues	14064-D The St. Louis Blues / Cold in Hand Blues
	14195-D Back-Water Blues / Preachin' the Blues	14075-D The Yellow Dog Blues / Soft Pedal Blues
	14137-D Hard Drivin' Papa / Money Blues	

SMITH, CLARA—Vocal

14419-D Got My Mind on That Thing / Gin Mill Blues

SMITH, KATE—Vocal

56000-D Kate Smith Presents a Memory Program / Ted Lewis Presents a Miniature Dance Program	2624-D Snuggled on Your Shoulder / Love, You Funny Thing!	
18000-D Medley—"Face the Music" F.T. Ben Selvin Orch. with Kate Smith, Jack Miller and the Three Nitecaps	2605-D Twenty-One Years / In the Baggage Coach Ahead	
	2563-D That's Why Darkies Were Born / Tell Me with a Love Song	

a group called The Famous Hokum Boys that included Georgia Tom and a guitarist called Big Bill Broonzy. Big Bill had had two rather disappointing records issued by Paramount in 1928, and now ARC recorded five solo items by him, and issued them under the name Sammy Sampson. Bill sang straight country blues numbers, with less recourse to *double-entendre* than most singers of the period, and provided complex, rhythmic guitar accompaniments. In September 1930 ARC had a second race recording session – involving once again Georgia Tom, Sammy Sampson and the Famous Hokum Boys. The next year they went slightly further afield, and recorded twenty-one gospel numbers by the Famous Garland Jubilee Singers, ten sermons by former Paramount artist Rev Emmet Dickinson, twenty blues by Gennett's Sam Collins (including *I'm Still Sitting On Top Of The World*) and eighteen numbers by Joe Evans and Arthur McClain, guitarist-singers from Alabama who affected a Mississippi Sheiks style, and even added a violin for *their* version of *Sitting On Top Of The World*. In 1931 and into 1932 ARC issued a steady two records or so each month by their limited group of artists, in the Perfect 100 series. All the records were also simultaneously issued on Oriole, Romeo and – from the end of 1931 – on Banner. Thus Perfect 0189, by the Famous Garland Jubilee Singers, was also on Oriole 8088, Romeo 5088 and Banner 32266; Perfect 0193 by Sam Collins (labelled as Salty Dog Sam) came out on Oriole 8106, Romeo 5106 and Banner 32311. While the Perfect series contained

ORIOLE RECORDS

Old Familiar Tunes—Sacreds and Race

(Ready For Shipment November 1st)   Oct. 22, 1931.

OLD TIME SINGING and PLAYING

8100 (TWENTY-ONE YEARS   Vocal-Nov.Acc.   Carson Robison Trio
     (IN THE CUMBERLAND MOUNTAINS   Vocal-Nov.Acc.   Carson Robison Trio
This is a national hit, TWENTY-ONE YEARS - the prison song of the south, the song that
everyone is singing. "I've Counted The Footsteps, I've Counted The Stars, I've Counted A Million Of These Prison Bars." It happened in Nashville, Tenn. A real master-
piece. Buy this record in quantity lots -- you'll sell plenty. It is coupled with
"In The Cumberland Mountains", another wonderful number, a song that speaks for itself.

8101 (DARLING NELLIE GRAY   Vocal Duet-Nov.Acc.   Martin & Roberts
     (SUNNY TENNESSEE   Vocal Duet-Nov.Acc.   Martin & Roberts
These numbers are nationally known and are recorded by genuine southern talent. A
title strip announcing this record and proper demonstration will result in sales.

8102 (THE LITTLE OLD JAIL HOUSE   Vocal   Asa Martin
     (THE ROVING MOONSHINER   Vocal   Asa Martin
The "Jailhouse" and the "Moonshiner" are two subjects that will always sell. They are
recorded by talent who lives with them and renders them in their own inimitable style.
Don't overlook Martin's story about the Jailhouse and the Moonshiner.

8103 (I SHALL NOT BE MOVED   Vocal Duet   Frank & James McCravy
     (METHODIST PIE   Vocal-Nov.Acc.   Gene Autry
Two songs that are known by everyone and recorded by artists who have a tremendous
following.

8104 (THE WAGGONER   Old Time Fiddling   Fiddling Doc Roberts Trio
     (SHORTENIN' BREAD   Old Time Fiddling   Fiddling Doc Roberts Trio
Two 'hot' fiddle tunes that are sure-fire. Doc Roberts, the champion old time fiddler,
puts these numbers over in a style that is pleasing to all lovers of old time dance
tunes. You'll sell plenty of this record -- keep a supply on hand.

BLUES by COLORED ARTISTS

8105 (AIN'T GOING THERE NO MORE   Vocal-Inst.Acc.   'Famous' Hokum Boys
     (PIE EATING STRUT   Vocal-Inst.Acc.   'Famous' Hokum Boys
Every colored person knows the Famous Hokum Boys. This record is true to their style.
It has plenty of snap and just the type the negro looks for.

8106 (SLOW MAMA SLOW   Vocal with Guitar   Salty Dog Sam
     (NEW SALTY DOG   Vocal with Guitar   Salty Dog Sam
These two songs are recorded by a new artist "just from the South". Genuine negro
blues in the style the negro likes. There is a big demand for this type of selection.
This is your chance to clean up. A down home record by a down home artist. Be sure
to demonstrate this record to every negro that comes to your counter. Tell them it is
made by a real negro. This is a real big opportunity.

8107 (BLACK CAT CROSSED YOUR PATH   Sermon   Rev. Jordan Jones & Cong.
     (HELL AND WHAT IT IS   Sermon   Rev. Jordan Jones & Cong.
This record will be bought by white people as well as negroes. The subject is true to
negro superstition, they will like it and the white people will buy it for the kick
they get out of it.

American Record Corporation   **1776 Broadway, N.Y.**

*An ARC advance release sheet circulated to its dealers, Rev. Jordan
Jones was a pseudonym for Rev Emmet Dickinson. Left: Georgia Tom.*

only race records, Romeo and Oriole bore hillbilly as well, and Banner featured a full range of popular material, in addition to race and hillbilly. All the labels were priced at 25 cents, but sold through different retail outlets – Romeo could only be bought in S. H. Kress's dime stores, Oriole only in McCrory's stores, and so on. They became known, collectively, as 'the dime store labels'.

In April 1930, Brunswick-Balke-Collender's record division had been bought by Warner Brothers Pictures. The name was changed to the Brunswick Radio Corporation and the headquarters moved from Chicago to New York, but otherwise everything was as it had been. With the gradual rundown of Paramount, BRC was undisputed leader of the race market. Not only did they have Tampa Red and Leroy Carr: in Memphis, in February 1930, Vocalion had recorded some solo blues and some duets by singer-guitarists Memphis Minnie and her husband Kansas Joe McCoy. Columbia had recorded them in New York in 1929, but didn't even issue all the titles they had made. Now, Vocalion made a big thing of Minnie's earthy singing and classic guitar accompaniment. Her big tune was *Bumble Bee*, issued on Vocalion 1476 about May 1930; when Columbia saw how well it was selling they belatedly – in August 1930 – issued the version they had recorded fourteen months previously. Vocalion followed up with *Bumble Bee No. 2*, on Vocalion 1556 in January '31, and *New Bumble Bee*, on 1618 in July. The theme was simple:

> I've got a bumble bee
> Don't sting nobody but me
> And I tell the world
> He's got all the things I need

Memphis Minnie and Kansas Joe appeared on fourteen records in 1931 – there were six solo blues by Joe, six duets, and sixteen solos by Minnie.

BRC were the only company to issue as many blues and gospel items in 1931 as they had the previous year. In addition to nearly a hundred in the Vocalion 1000 series, they produced around forty on Brunswick. The 7000 series had the slogan 'Get 'em – cause they're HOT!', but it contained nothing as hot as Memphis Minnie. Lucille Bogan – the first singer to have been recorded on location – now had regular releases on Brunswick; she had improved enormously since 1923 and on two records her full voice and perfect phrasing were admirably complemented by Tampa

Red's guitar. Warner discontinued field trips at the end of 1930, and about the same time they started a cheap label – Melotone. The 500 records put out on Melotone in its first two years only included a score of race items, amongst them three popular religious items that had appeared on Vocalion in 1927 – a Blind Joe Taggart, Edward W. Clayborn's first record, and Rev A. W. Nix's *Black Diamond Express To Hell*, Parts 1 and 2.

In October 1930 Consolidated Film Industries had bought ARC; then, in December 1931, they purchased the Brunswick Record Corporation from Warner Brothers. ARC and BRC maintained separate identities on the surface – as sister subsidiaries within the CFI organisation – but they were effectively run as one concern. The Brunswick 7000 race series was discontinued (it had reached 7233) and although the Vocalion 1000's were continued, the price was reduced from 75 cents to 35 cents. New titles from Tampa Red and Memphis Minnie were put out both on Vocalion and on

ROMEO RECORDS
by
AMERICA'S BEST RACE ARTISTS
BLUES — SACREDS — SPIRITUALS

25c 25c

BIG BILL

5494	{ I Wanta See My Baby / Hobo Blues	5-11-67	{ Rising Sun, Shine On / Let Her Go — / She Don't Know
5433	{ Prowlin' Ground Hog / C-C Rider		
5347	{ Mistreating Mama Blues / Long Tall Mama	35-10-31	{ Dirty No-Gooder / Dying Day Blues

— FOR SALE BY —

S. H. KRESS 5, 10 and 25c Stores

72

ARC's four dime store labels, selling at 25 cents. Big Bill was now being issued under his own name, but just on the dime store labels. ARC-BRC's control of the market can be seen from the fact that in 1932 they had three of the four most popular artists (in terms of number of releases) – Tampa Red, Memphis Minnie and Big Bill; the one they didn't have was the Mississippi Sheiks, who appeared that year on OKeh, Columbia and Paramount.

But sales were *still* falling. In April 1932, $100 was paid for twenty tunes from Joshua White, a singer who had been Blind Joe Taggart's lead boy at the age of thirteen, and who had recorded with him for Paramount. This was ARC-BRC's last race recording of the year. Even when the field unit visited San Antonio in November only hillbilly artists were used. Material that had already been recorded continued to be put in the Vocalion 1000 series until it ran out in November. In mid-1933 a few items by ARC artists were issued on Vocalion under pseudonym – Joshua White became Tippy Barton, for instance – and the series finally finished with number 1745, by Big Bill.

Regular issues continued to be made on Perfect, Romeo, Oriole and Banner – and from November 1932 all material was also issued simultaneously on Melotone. Some recording was done in 1933 – a group of Georgia singers including Buddy Moss, Curly Weaver and Blind Willie McTell, Lucille Bogan, and a few more. Surprisingly, no recordings were made in 1933 of the most popular singers from the immediately preceding years: Tampa Red, Leroy Carr, Memphis Minnie and Big Bill. In the late summer of '33 BRC started a new Vocalion general series, the 2500s. At first there were few race issues – the Blind Willie McTell titles, and some numbers by Lucille Bogan's guitarist, Sonny Scott. However, by the end of the year sales were improving and in 1934, for the first time since 1931, ARC-BRC recorded race artists in Chicago – including Tampa Red and Memphis Minnie. And they also travelled to St Louis to record Leroy Carr and Scrapper Blackwell. Things were getting back to normal at Vocalion.

But not so at Columbia. Although ARC-BRC were finding a market for their 35 cent and 25 cent discs, people were still loth to spend 75 cents on a Columbia or OKeh record. Finally Grigsby-Grunow went into liquidation and in late 1934 BRC bought its subsidiary, the Columbia Phonograph Company. In 1923 there had been a dozen independent labels issuing race records. Through an eleven-year sequence of merger and take-over, seven of these – Brunswick, Vocalion, Cameo, Banner, Perfect, OKeh and Colum-

Above: Crying Blues *was also issued on Perfect 0234, Romeo 5240, Oriole 8240 and Banner 32794. Right: A Victor advertising supplement, early 1930.*

bia – were now owned by Consolidated Film Industries.

Victor, who had been taken over by the Radio Corporation of America in January 1929, were the only company successfully to weather the depression years without change of ownership. Their sales were as low as anyone else's – and in 1932 industry sales were six million discs, as compared with 104 million in 1927. But Victor's resources were more solid and, as hard times worsened, they effected a policy of ruthless economy. At first, the company had tried to fight off falling sales. Although Victor had issued race catalogues and supplements in the peak years they had not advertised in the black press. Then, in March 1930 there was a Victor display in the *Chicago Defender,* the first since August 1923;

this was in fact the month before Paramount stopped advertising in the *Defender*. However, sales continued to fall and the nineteenth Victor insertion – on 27th December 1930 – was the last.

Like the other major companies Victor had always made at least two 'takes' of each title. This was an obvious point for economy, and on 16th June 1931 Raymond R. Sooy, the chief recording engineer, sent round a memorandum 'Starting with this date, only one wax to be processed, unless wax becomes defective'. In 1931, with country blues selling less and less well, Victor decided to dispense with their annual visit to Memphis. In May they called at Charlotte, North Carolina, mainly for hillbilly material, and went on to Louisville, where they recorded the white singer Jimmie Rodgers, and also a number of blues piano sides by Walter Davis and Roosevelt Sykes. Sykes had been discovered by talent scout Jesse Johnson in 1929, and taken to New York to record, as OKeh's answer to Leroy Carr. Since he was under contract to OKeh, Sykes told Victor that his name was Willie Kelly, and his records were issued thus. Walter Davis's mellow vocal style and Carr-like material were liked, and he was again recorded by Victor in Chicago in September.

In 1931 Victor cut their blues and gospel releases by a third, to about forty. They had discontinued the V38500 series – at V38631 – the previous year and in January '31 started a 23250 blues and gospel series (there was also a 23000 series for jazz, and a 23500 one for hillbilly material). The only race recordings Victor made in 1932 were in the course of their single field trip, to Dallas and Atlanta in February. They went to Dallas for Jimmie Rodgers, and also recorded Walter Davis and a few local blues singers; in Atlanta there were four tunes from the inevitable Blind Willie McTell and four blues duets from the Sparks brothers, issued as 'Pinetop and Lindberg'. Most of the material from this trip had been issued by the middle of the year, and thereafter Victor continued to put out race records simply by using titles that they had recorded three or four years before, and rejected at the time. Three-quarters of the selections issued between summer '32 and summer '33 had been recorded at least two years earlier – there was a Frank Stokes from 1929, a Robert Wilkins from '28, a Memphis Jug Band from '29, and so on.

In 1931 total blues and gospel releases had averaged eight a week, only twenty per cent below the level of the peak years. In 1932 they were half that, and the following year there were less than 150 new issues – the lowest level since 1922. In 1933 Victor were still charging 75 cents – and that for material that they had considered below par years before. With unemployment running high few black or white customers could afford this price. In order to survive, Victor were forced to follow ARC-BRC and enter the cheap record market. Their 35 cent label, Bluebird, was launched in the summer of 1933. The first race discs on Bluebird were reissues of old Victor material – by Walter Davis, the Memphis Jug Band, Cannon's Jug Stompers and Rev Gates. But Victor needed new material, and they decided to go to Chicago to find it.

In the 'twenties, Victor had seldom recorded more than eight titles in a day, whereas most companies had averaged twice as many. There was time for an artist to discuss his material with the recording manager, rehearse it thoroughly, and then record it twice at a leisurely pace. Even after the company started making one and not two takes of each tune, in 1931, ten titles was a good day's work. Now, as a further economy, engineers were told to make maximum use of the studio facilities and their own time. Thus, on Wednesday 2nd August 1933, no less than thirty-five race titles were recorded in Chicago, by a dozen artists including Roosevelt Sykes (once more as Willie Kelly), the Sparks brothers, and Walter Davis. The Walter Davis items were put out simultaneously on Bluebird, at 35 cents, and in the Victor 23250 series, at 75 cents. However, it soon became apparent that there was little point in continuing to produce 75 cent race records and at the end of 1933 the Victor race series – which had reached 23432 – was withdrawn.

By the beginning of 1934 there were, besides the ailing and barely active Gennett and Columbia concerns, only two companies competing for the race market: ARC-BRC and Victor. But that year there emerged a strong new competitor. In the middle of the year, English Decca financed an American company of the same name and put in charge Jack Kapp, who had run Brunswick-Balke-Collender's race series. Even more important, Jack Kapp brought with him Mayo Williams, as race talent scout. They began recording in New York and Chicago in August and before the end of the year had issued two or three dozen items in their new race series, the Decca 7000's. Whereas the other two companies still maintained 75 cent labels (Victor and Brunswick respectively) in addition to the cheap Bluebird and Vocalion, Decca priced all their records at 35 cents; to cut overheads they began by making just one take of each title. Decca intended to grab as large a share as it could of the once more expanding record market.

URBAN BLUES
1934-1940

From 1934 until 1945 there were three main race labels, all selling at 35 cents: Decca, the Brunswick Record Corporation's Vocalion, and RCA-Victor's Bluebird. Whereas Decca had a special race series, Bluebird and Vocalion numbered blues and gospel material in their general series. However, Vocalion added an 0- prefix to the number of each hillbilly and race item in the 2500 series. And although the Bluebird B5000 series at first featured all types of music, after B7950 (at the end of 1938) this series was reserved for hillbilly and race material, with popular records transferred to the new B10000 series.

Gennett had failed at the end of 1934. On 28th June 1935 Decca bought the Champion trademark, and rights to certain Gennett material. Late that year they started their second race series, the Champion 50000s; it featured some reissues of Gennett blues – including the final four sides by Frank James – and some reissues from Paramount – including all twelve tunes from the Mississippi Sheiks's 1932 session – as well as original material recorded by Decca. However, the series cannot have been a success, for it was discontinued after only seventy-eight issues. After BRC bought the Columbia Phonograph Corporation, in late 1934, they put out a further thirteen records in the OKeh 8000 series – newly recorded selections by Papa Charlie Jackson and the Memphis Jug Band, favourites of seven years before. Papa Charlie recorded a new version of *Skoodle-um-skoo*, on OKeh 8954. The Memphis Jug Band's *Jug Band Quartette* and *Little Green Slippers*, on OKeh 8966, was the last issue in the 8000 series; it had lasted for fourteen years, longer than any other race series.

Besides its regular Vocalion issues, BRC-ARC were also putting out race records on the five 'dime store labels' – Perfect, Oriole, Romeo, Banner and Melotone – still selling at 25 cents. Generally, the dime store labels did not duplicate material that had appeared on Vocalion. In late 1935, ARC replaced the complicated numbering system (which had been different for each label) with an extremely simple system. The first part of the number indicated the year, the second part the month, and the third part the

number of the individual record in that month's batch of releases, popular records being numbered from 1 and hillbilly and race from 51. Every, or almost every, number appeared on each of the five labels. Thus Big Bill's *C & A Blues* was on 5–12–65; it was the fifteenth hillbilly/race disc issued in December 1935.

There was one change of company ownership in the late 'thirties. In February 1938 the Columbia Broadcasting System bought BRC-ARC. Within two months they had discontinued the five dime store labels; before the end of the year they followed Victor's example of 1931 and told their engineers to make one, and not two, takes of each title; then, in 1940, they changed the name of their expensive label from Brunswick to Columbia, and of the cheaper one from Vocalion to OKeh. All records after 5621 were put out as OKeh; some of the better-selling earlier records in the 2500 series – originally put out as Vocalion – were re-pressed as OKehs.

There were two other labels that featured a fair quantity of race material during the 'thirties. The store group Montgomery Ward, with a label of the same name, drew at various times on Gennett, Decca and Bluebird. And Sears Roebuck used ARC material on its Conqueror label; the Sears catalogue priced Conqueror records at 21 cents each in 1934, at two for 45 cents in late 1935, and at the bargain price of six for 55 cents in the autumn of '36.

The urban style of music that had appeared – notably on BBC's Vocalion – at the very end of the 'twenties dominated the market from 1934 on. Tampa Red, Memphis Minnie, Big Bill, Roosevelt Sykes and Walter Davis each continued to have a new record issued every few weeks until the beginning of the war. Leroy Carr died in 1935, and the following year Decca issued nine records by Bill Gaither, a black radio store proprietor from Louisville, under the name 'Leroy's Buddy'. Gaither played guitar, and sang very much in Leroy's style; his piano player,

Honey Hill, imitated Leroy, and Gaither's records sold well for half-a-dozen years.

In 1934 Mayo Williams was managing two artists who had been briefly featured in the Vocalion 1000 series a few years earlier: Amos Easton, who wasn't very proficient on any instrument but sang well in the easy, relaxed manner of Leroy Carr, and Peetie Wheatstraw, who was as fluent on guitar as he was on piano and whose singing had more bite and vigour than Easton's. The race labels were anxious for new talent and in 1934 Williams arranged for Easton to record for all three of the major labels; most of his records appear under the pseudonym 'Bumble Bee Slim'.

Both Victor and BRC-ARC sent out field units in 1934. Victor contacted the perennial Rev Gates in Atlanta, but otherwise the race activity was in Texas. BRC-ARC recorded the old OKeh singer Texas Alexander in San Antonio in April and again in Fort Worth in September; in March Victor visited San Antonio to record Bo Carter and the Mississippi Sheiks and a new artist called Joe Pullum. Pullum didn't play any instrument but he sang, in an almost falsetto voice, with incredible control and feeling; he was perhaps the most technically accomplished of all blues singers. Rob Cooper's barrelhouse piano accompaniment perfectly reinforced and complemented Pullum's vocal. Their first record, on Bluebird B5459, was *Black Gal What Makes Your Head So Hard?*:

> Black gal, black gal
> What makes your head so hard?
> Black gal, woman what makes your head so hard?
> Lord, I would come to see you
> But your man has got me barred

Pullum's record was such a success that Vocalion had no less an artist than Leroy Carr record *Black Gal*, in New York in August. Within a few weeks of opening their Chicago studio, Decca got Mary Johnson to record the tune (issued on Decca 7014); then, as Bluebird exploited their success by putting out Pullum singing *Black Gal*, nos. 2, 3 and 4 (on B5592, B5844 and B5947) Decca recorded another version by a rather mediocre singer called Jimmie Gordon. When Decca issued Gordon's *Black Gal* on 7043 the label read 'Joe Bullum'! However, they afterwards repented of the subterfuge and relabelled the record as by Jimmie Gordon.

Pullum's popularity waned fairly soon and Bluebird stopped recording him in 1936. Record buyers preferred the rocking beat of the Chicago artists to Pullum's quiet, introspective approach. Even Big Bill was now using a piano player, and a drummer or bass player, and gradually forsaking his country blues origins for a swinging, urban sound. Will Weldon, who had been on the Memphis Jug Band's first records, came back in 1935 to make his first recordings in eight years; Weldon, styling himself Casey Bill, played a steel guitar with panache and sounded very much like Tampa Red. Vocalion even got Big Bill and Casey Bill together, and labelled the records 'The Hokum Boys'. Casey Bill was managed by Lester Melrose, the brother of Frank Melrose (a white pianist who played in such a Negroid manner that he had had a record in the old Paramount race series). Melrose also managed Lil Johnson, whose full voice and controlled phrasing were reminiscent of the best of the classic blues singers. The only other popular woman singer – apart from Memphis Minnie – was Georgia White, who was also a lively pianist and was billed by Decca as 'The World's Greatest Blues Singer'.

When the companies began full-scale recording again, in 1934, they were each after the most popular artists; and the singers sometimes took advantage of the situation. In 1934 Amos Easton had twelve records issued, on Bluebird, Decca and Vocalion. His popularity was at its height and the following year, still contriving to record for all the companies, he had no less than twenty-nine releases (including some, under the pseudonym Shelley Armstrong, on Decca's second-string Champion label) – twelve more than any one blues singer had ever had issued in one year before. In 1935 half the best-selling artists were recording for at least two companies. But the companies soon introduced some order, by insisting on exclusive contracts; by 1938 each of the most popular artists was firmly tied to just one label. Of course people sometimes tried to get around it. Lester Melrose managed several of the major blues singers and many minor ones. In 1937 he took over, from Mayo Williams, a new rough-voiced singer from Mississippi called Johnnie Temple. Melrose arranged a Decca contract for Temple and then, in October 1937, took him to the Vocalion studio. However, soon after the session Vocalion noticed that Decca were making regular issues of Temple's records. Decca confirmed that their contract with Temple did not expire until 21st May 1939; Vocalion made a file memorandum against the four Temple titles 'do not release', and – on 6th June 1938 –

Joe Pullum, from the 1937 Bluebird catalogue.

Melrose refunded the $84 he had received for the session the previous October.

Industry sales were steadily rising: thirty-seven million discs were sold in 1937, six times as many as five years before. More and more blues and gospel records were released every year. From a less-than-three-a-week average in 1933, with many of these being titles recorded years before, issues gradually increased until in 1937 the average was nine a week. The total for 1937 was

DECCA
RACE RECORDS

DECCA

The Country's Greatest Artists

THE HONEY DRIPPER

OLLIE SHEPARD

ROSETTA HOWARD

PEETIE WHEATSTRAW

NORFOLK Jubilee Quartet

GEORGIA WHITE

SLEEPY JOHN ESTES

**BLUES SINGING · BLUES DANCE · HOT DANCE
SACRED · PREACHING**

fifty less than the annual output during the peak years, but in fact the number of blues records was about the same (just under 400); the difference was in the number of gospel releases.

Gospel issues had been cut back even more than blues in the hard years of '32 and '33; and there was no big increase in religious recordings from 1934 onwards, as there was with blues. Sermons were virtually out. Bluebird recorded Rev Gates in 1934 and then not again until 1939; Decca brought back Rev J. C. Burnett for eight titles in 1938. But this was almost all; there were usually only about half-a-dozen sermon records in any year after 1931. In fact, of the 370 sermon discs issued in the period covered by this book – nearly 100 of these being by Rev Gates – more than 300 were put out between mid-1926 and the end of 1931.

In 1934 there was some recording of guitar evangelists. Joshua White made a number of sacred items, and after a while ARC kept his own name for religious records, putting out blues numbers under the pseudonym Pinewood Tom. In 1934 Decca brought back Blind Joe Taggart and the following year they recorded a number of gospel songs from Blind Willie McTell, and even persuaded Memphis Minnie to sing *Let Me Ride* and *When The Saints Go Marching Home* – issued on Decca 7063 as by Gospel Minnie. But there were fewer records by guitar evangelists being released than during the peak years, and soon even these faded away; in 1938 there was not a single new issue.

The main religious activity in the 'thirties concerned gospel quartets. In 1934 there had only been eight quartet records, but the number gradually built up until in 1938 there were over fifty, the level of the peak years. Every label had its regular quartet – Mitchell's Christian Singers on Vocalion, the Heavenly Gospel Singers on Bluebird, and Paramount's Norfolk Jubilee Quartet on Decca.

The companies had three main ways of unearthing new talent. By placing advertisements in local papers, especially just before a field unit was due in a nearby town; by just relying on chance comments from singers, concerning others who might be good recording propositions; and by employing their own talent scouts, who would carry out steady, systematic searches. The last method was intensively employed in the 'thirties – Roosevelt Sykes, for

The cover of Decca's 1938 catalogue; 'The Honey Dripper' was pianist Roosevelt Sykes.

instance, would find likely artists for Decca (or sometimes, for Lester Melrose). But despite this, race catalogues in the 'thirties relied more heavily on a small nucleus of popular singers than they had in the 'twenties. In 1937, sixteen singers had more than six records issued in the year, accounting altogether for more than a third of all race releases; in the peak years there had usually been about ten artists with more than six records out in a year, and they altogether accounted for less than a fifth of the total releases.

There was far less recording in the field in the 'thirties; in view of the popularity of the Chicago singers there was less need. Decca in fact seem to have gone south only once – to New Orleans in March 1936, when they recorded some cajun artists and two blues singers: Walter Vincson, of the Mississippi Sheiks, and Oscar Woods, 'The Lone Wolf'. Victor made about four field trips a year, mainly for the hillbilly catalogue. They dropped the Mississippi Sheiks in 1935 but continued to record a dozen new titles by Bo Carter every year, or every other year, calling him to San Antonio, New Orleans or Atlanta. In 1935 Victor recorded four titles in New Orleans by Little Brother Montgomery, an original and versatile pianist with a highly personal whining vocal style. He sang one of his own compositions, that had been featured on his single Paramount release, in 1930:

> I've got the Vicksburg blues, and I'm singing them
>   everywhere I go (*twice*)
> Now the reason I sing them, my baby says she don't
>   want me no more

Vicksburg Blues, on Bluebird B6072, was a success and the following year Victor returned to New Orleans to record more titles by Brother, and some by other local singers.

Whereas in the 'twenties Victor had normally recorded eight titles a day in the field (while the competition would do fifteen to twenty), they now aimed at twenty-five or more (the competition still stuck to between fifteen and twenty). In the St Charles Hotel, New Orleans, on Thursday, 15th October 1936, they began with twelve duets from the Chatman Brothers (who were in fact two of Bo Carter's brothers, Chatman being his real name). Then four from Matilda Powell, calling herself Mississippi Matilda. Between 4.45 and 6 p.m. they recorded six tunes by Eugene Powell (presumably some relation of Matilda), under the name

The 1940 Decca catalogue; 'Leroy's Buddy' was Bill Gaither.

Sonny Boy Nelson. Then, into the evening, they recorded eight harmonica blues by Robert Hill, with Eugene Powell providing guitar accompaniment; and then twelve blues from Bo Carter. Bo Carter received twenty percent of Sonny Boy Nelson's royalty – presumably he acted as Nelson's agent – and his address was recorded as c/o Matilda Powell, Anguilla, Mississippi, showing the close connections between all these artists. The next day the unit began with twelve blues from Tommy Griffin; then four from Annie Turner, with Little Brother Mongomery accompanying on the piano; then no less than eighteen tunes, one after another, from Little Brother; after that a sentimental song from Creole George Guesnon, again accompanied by Little Brother; and finally two numbers from Walter Vincson (going under the name Walter Jacobs). They had recorded eighty-one tunes in two days – what would have been a normal two weeks' work six years earlier. The New Orleans session in 1936 was Victor's last substantial race field recording; in subsequent years they recorded a fair number of gospel quartets in the field, but only one or two unimportant blues singers.

By and large Victor visited the same towns over and over again – New Orleans, San Antonio, Atlanta and Charlotte, North Carolina. BRC-ARC, however, took pains to seek out talent in unusual places. In 1935 they visited Jackson, Mississippi; in 1936 Augusta, Georgia and Hattiesburg, Mississippi; and in 1937 Hot Springs, Arkansas and Birmingham, Alabama. They recorded about a hundred titles at each location of which rather more than half were generally by black artists. Some fine country blues singers were recorded, including Robert Wilkins, who had been featured on Brunswick and Victor in the 'twenties (this time he gave his name as Tim Wilkins). But there was really little demand for country blues in the 'thirties, and the company didn't even bother to issue a large proportion of the material they collected.

BRC-ARC made regular visits to San Antonio and Dallas (though never to Atlanta) for hillbilly material, and also did some useful blues recording there. In 1935 and 1936 they recorded a group of artists put forward by local talent spotter Lester Hearne, including pianist Black Boy Shine and singer Bernice Edwards. In 1937 the white singer Jimmie Davis (who later became Governor of Louisiana) suggested Kitty Gray and her Wampus Cats, a Texas group with something of a Chicago sound, but featuring the Shreveport guitarist Oscar Woods. At the same session – in San Antonio – Vocalion recorded six sides each by

Son Becky and Pinetop Burks; the latter especially was a brilliant pianist-singer in the best Texas tradition. And in San Antonio the company recorded a young country blues singer whose records did sell well – Robert Johnson, from Mississippi, who brought an unusual tortured intensity to his singing and bottle-neck guitar playing. BRC-ARC recorded sixteen tunes by Johnson in November 1936, and then a further thirteen in Dallas the next June. This was Johnson's last session; he was said to have been poisoned by his girl friend soon after it.

There were two other country blues singers who could hold their own against Tampa Red, Bumble Bee Slim and the rest in the race lists of the 'thirties: Sleepy John Estes, who had been a Victor artist in '29 and '30 and now had regular releases in the

Sleepy John Estes' original blues were featured on 15 records in the Decca race series.

Decca 7000 series, and Blind Boy Fuller, an itinerant singer-guitarist from Carolina. Fuller was first recorded by Vocalion in 1935 and his clear, mean-sounding voice and accomplished, rhythmic guitar style gradually became more and more popular. In July 1937 Decca recorded twelve blues by Fuller and immediately issued four of them on Decca 7330 and 7331. But Vocalion protested that he had an exclusive contract with them and Decca were forced to withdraw the records; they were finally able to release them in 1942, after Fuller had died. In 1938 Blind Boy Fuller had fourteen records issued, more than any other artist – one more in fact than Big Bill, who had a new release each month throughout the 'thirties. The following year Columbia, who had bought the Vocalion label, got him to sing some religious numbers and issued them as by 'Brother George and his Sanctified Singers'; the Sanctified Singers were harmonica player Sonny Terry and Oh Red, Fuller's regular washboard accompanist. After Fuller's death, Columbia continued to use the name Brother George for records by another Carolina singer, Brownie McGhee, some of whose secular items were labelled – much to his annoyance – 'Blind Boy Fuller No 2'.

In 1937, the best year for blues since 1930, Lonnie Johnson returned to recording. And Bluebird began regular issues by two new Chicago stars: harmonica player and singer Sonny Boy Williamson, and Robert Brown, who went under the name Washboard Sam. Brown was a Lester Melrose protégé, and in 1935 and 1936 had had records issued on Vocalion under the names 'Ham Gravy' and 'Shufflin' Sam' as well as 'Washboard Sam'. Bluebird had issued one record in '35 and three in '36. Then, in 1937, they put out Bluebird B7001, *We Gonna Move* coupled with *Back Door*:

> Oh, tell me mama, who's that a while ago (*twice*)
> Yes, when I come in, who's that went out that back door

Sam did everything the Chicago singers had been doing for the past few years; and he did it better. His powerful rhythmic vocal – backed by Big Bill's guitar, Black Bob's piano, Sam's own agile washboard, and Arnett Nelson's fluid clarinet – was irresistible. Bluebird arranged an exclusive contract and Washboard Sam, too, had a new release every month.

Washboard Sam, perhaps the most popular singer of the late '30's.

LONNIE JOHNSON, Blues Singer

B-8322 { Nothing But a Rat / She's My Mary

B-8338 { Four O Three Blues / The Loveless Blues

B-8363 { Why Women Go Wrong / She's Only a Woman

B-8387 { Trust Your Husband / Jersey Belle Blues

B-8530 { Get Yourself Together / Don't Be No Fool

B-8564 { Be Careful / I'm Just Dumb

Lonnie Johnson recorded for over forty years. He was featured on OKeh from 1925 until 1932, on Decca in 1937 and 1938, on Bluebird from 1939 to 1944 (shown here), on the Cincinnatti label King around 1950, and on Bluesville LPs in the early '60's.

Tampa Red was still recording steadily for Bluebird, and Memphis Minnie for Vocalion. Minnie was paid at the flat-rate of $12.50 per side. And she could reckon to be doing well: another Vocalion artist, pianist Curtis Jones, received only $7.50 per side. When the company took a field unit to Memphis, in July 1939, their rates were even lower. The company files show total expenses of $67.55 for ten tunes by singer-guitarist Little Buddy Doyle – $5 per side for Doyle, $10 overall for Hammie Nix, who accompanied on the harmonica, and $7.55 for expenses. Victor's rates at this time are not known, but they probably paid a little more. Decca's remuneration would have been about the same as

7315 Raggedy But Right
7375 Say Pretty Mama
7375 Slocum Blues

SMITH'S BURNING BUSH CONGREGATION, REV. NATHAN
(Religious Services with Singing)
7148 Baptism At Burning Bush
7150 Collection Time
7150 Joining Church
7148 Lord's Supper

SMITH'S BURNING BUSH SUNDAY SCHOOL PUPILS, REV. NATHAN
(Preaching with Singing)
7112 Burning Bush Sunday School (2 Parts)

SMITH, TRIXIE
(Blues Singing)
7489 Freight Train Blues
7528 He May Be Your Man
7528 Jack I'm Mellow
7469 My Daddy Rocks Me
7617 My Daddy Rocks Me—No. 2
7489 My Unusual Man
7617 No Good Man
7469 Trixie Blues

SMITH, WILLIE ("THE LION") and HIS CUBS
7086 Breeze—FT
7090 Echo of Spring—FT
7074 Harlem Joys—FT
7086 Sitting At The Table Opposite You—FT
7074 Streamline Gal—FT
7090 Swing, Brother, Swing—FT
7073 There's Gonna Be The Devil To Pay—FT
7073 What Can I Do With A Foolish Little Girl Like You—FT

SMITH'S JUBILEE SINGERS, WM. HENRY
7649 This Old Hammer Killed John Henry
7649 Time Is Drawing Nigh

SNEED, JACK, and HIS SNEEZERS
(Blues Singing)
7522 Big Joe Louis
7522 Numbers Man
7621 Ole Chris
7621 Paul Revere
7566 Sly Mongoose
7566 West Indies Blues

SPARTANBURG FAMOUS FOUR
(Gospel Singing)
7478 Anybody In Heaven That You Know
7476 Can You Make It to the City
7467 Do You Call That Religion
7468 Go Where I Send Thee
7468 Graveyard Is Waiting On Poor Me
7517 I Know My Time Ain't Long
7478 John Don't You Write No More
7543 John Wrote the Revelations
7543 Lilly of the Valley
7517 When That First Trumpet Sounds

SPIVEY, VICTORIA
7203 Black Snake Blues—FT
7204 Double Dozens—FT VC
7237 410 Blues

7204 Grievin' Me—FT VC
7203 I'll Never Fall In Love Again—FT VC
7222 Sweet Peace—FT VC
7222 T.B.'s Got Me—Blues
7237 You Weren't True—FT VC

SPRINGBACK JAMES
(Blues Singing)
7091 Rusty Can Blues
7081 Springback James
7119 Stingaree Mama Blues
7119 Texas Heifer Blues

STRANGE, JIMMIE
(Singing Fox Trots)
7226 Yas Yas Yas
7284 Yas Yas Yas No. 2

STRAUSS, JOHNNIE
(Blues Singing)
7081 Hard Working Woman
7035 Old Market Street Blues
7081 Radio Broadcasting Blues
7035 St. Louis Johnnie Blues

STURGIS, RODNEY
(Blues Singing)
7579 Away From You
7550 Gal That Wrecked My Life
7579 So Good
7550 Toodle Loo On Down

TAMPA KID
(Blues Singing)
7278 Baby Please Don't Go
7278 Keep On Trying

TEMPLE, JOHNNIE
(Vocal with Inst. Acc.)
7583 Better Not Let My Good Gal Catch You Here
7547 Between Midnight and Dawn
7547 Big Leg Woman
7678 Cherry Ball
7643 Down in Mississippi
7316 East St. Louis Blues
7660 Evil Bad Woman
7599 Getting Old Blues
7643 Good Suzie
7583 Grinding Mill
7599 If I Could Holler
7573 Jelly Roll Bert
7678 Let's Get Together
7244 Louise Louise Blues
7564 Mississippi Woman's Blues
7337 New Louise Louise Blues
7244 New Vicksburg Blues
7316 Peepin' Through the Keyhole
7444 Pimple Blues
7416 Snapping Cat
7357 So Lonely and Blue
7660 Streamline Blues
7632 Sun Goes Down in Blood
7632 Up Today and Down Tomorrow
7573 What A Fool I've Been
7564 When the Breath Bids Your Girl Friend's Body Goodbye

TEMPLE, JOHNNIE, and HARLEM HAMFATS
(Blues Dance with Singing)
7456 County Jail Blues
7495 Every Dog Must Have His Day
7495 Fare You Well
7385 Gimme Some of That Yum Yum Yum—Blues—FT
7532 Gonna Ride 74
7385 Hoodoo Women—Blues FT
7416 Mama's Bad Luck Child—Blues FT

7444 Mean Baby Blues—Blues FT
7532 Stavin' Chain
7456 What Is That Smell Like Gravy

THEARD, LOVIN' SAM
(The Mad Comic)
(Blues Singing)
7025 Rubbin' on the Darned Old Thing
7025 That Rhythm Gal
7146 Till I Die

THOMAS, EARL
(Blues Singing)
7221 Bonus Men
7195 Burying Ground
7221 Rent Day Blues
7195 Sugar Girl Blues

THREE RIFFS
(Jo-Eddie-Greene)
(Vocal Trio with Orch.)
7634 Ace in the Hole
7634 It's a Killer Mr. Miller

THREE SHARPS AND A FLAT
(Vocal)
7561 I Ain't in Love No More—Blues
7561 I Am I Am Am Am—Blues
7569 I'm Through—Voc. FT
7569 Swinging in the Candy Store—Voc. FT

TOLBERT, SKEETS, and HIS GENTLEMEN OF SWING
7630 Bouncing of Rhythm—Jump FT
7669 Fine Piece of Meat—FT
7570 Get Up—Jump FT
7717 Harlem Ain't What It Usta Be
7717 Hole Holy Roly-Poly
7722 I Can't Go for You—FT-VC
7653 I'm Blowin' My Top—Blues Dance
7591 I've Lost My Head Over You—Blues
7653 Railroad Blues—Blues Dance
7570 Skin 'Em Back—Jump FT
7630 Stuffs Out—FT
7669 Swing Out—Inst. FT
7591 This Is The End—Blues
7722 W.P.A.—FT-VC

TREMER, GEORGE H.
(Piano Novelty)
7137 Spirit of '49 Rag

TRICE, RICH
(Blues Singing with Guitar)
7701 Come On Baby
7701 Trembling Bed Spring Blues

TRICE, WELLY
(Blues Singing)
7358 Come On In Here Mama
7358 Let Her Go God Bless Her

UNCLE JOE DOBSON
(Preaching with Singing)
7055 Kin You Take It
7124 My God is a Rock in the Weary Land
7124 There Was a Man
7055 You Wooden Pistol You

UNCLE SKIPPER
(Blues Singing)
7353 Chifferobe
7353 Cutting My A B C's
7455 Look What A Shape I'm In
7455 Twee Twee Twa

According to the 1940 Decca catalogue, every race record issued in the 7000 series was still available. Springback James was Frank James, who had recorded for Gennett in 1934. No one knows the real name of Tampa Kid, who gives a passable imitation of Tampa Red.

Vocalion's. It appears in fact that singers were now being paid rather less than they had been ten years before; when Mississippi John Hurt – a fairly unknown singer – was asked to come to New York to record by OKeh in 1928 he was paid $20 per side, in addition to all his expenses.

From '34 to '36 blues and gospel releases made up about twenty percent of the total issues of the three companies. With sales of pop records still disappointing, it was a worthwhile effort to cultivate the race market. Then pop interest revived; in 1937 there were twice as many pop issues as in the previous year. Race releases were about fifteen percent higher – Decca and Bluebird each put out around 120 items whilst BRC-ARC issued almost 100 on Vocalion, and another 100 on the dime store labels. When CBS bought BRC-ARC in early '38 they stopped production of the dime store labels, and, although a few more race records appeared on Vocalion than previously, there was an overall loss – blues and gospel releases in 1938 averaged less than eight a week, one a week down on '37. But in 1938 pop issues again doubled, and the companies began devoting more and more of their time to popular material, to the detriment of the race catalogue. Decca shut down their permanent studio in Chicago in May '37, and thereafter just went there once or twice a year, for a few days of intensive recording activity; CBS went to San Antonio in May 1938 and – for the first time since 1932 – did not record a single black artist. Blues and gospel releases were down to six a week by 1940. And an increasing proportion were gospel items – mostly unaccompanied quartets; a quarter of the total race releases in 1939 were sacred, as against an eighth two years earlier. Taking advantage of the boom, Victor recorded Rev Gates again in Rock Hill, South Carolina in February '39, and then in Atlanta in 1940.

In the post-'37 years most releases were by established artists: Blind Boy Fuller, Big Bill, Washboard Sam, Tampa Red, Bill Gaither, Walter Davis, Peetie Wheatstraw, Sonny Boy Williamson and so on (Bumble Bee Slim had been dropped in 1938). But there were a few innovations. For instance, four of the classic blues singers reappeared briefly – Black Swan's Trixie Smith and Paramount's Alberta Hunter recorded a few titles for Decca and Bluebird; Lester Melrose was instrumental in getting Victoria Spivey back into the studios; and jazz enthusiast John Hammond – who had arranged Bessie Smith's last session in 1933 – supervised a session involving Ida Cox and her All Star Orchestra, in the Columbia studios in 1940.

Rev. J. M. GATES and his Congregation

B-5033 {Adam and Eve in the Garden
Samson and the Woman

B-5111 {I Know I Got Religion
Funeral Train

B-5627 {Wolf Cat and His Catcher
New Dead Cat on the Line

B-5660 {There Is Something About the Lord Mighty Sweet
On the Battlefield

B-5703 {Highway Robbers in the Night
Don't Hide From Your Furniture Man

B-5725 {Will You Have Christmas Dinner in Jail
No Bad Streets in Town

B-5755 {Rev. Gates' Song Service
Valley of Death

B-5792 {Highway to Hell
Hell Ain't Half Full

B-5824 {Lord, I'm in Your Care
Goin' Through the Pearly Gates

B-5901 {Born to Die
Prepare to Meet Thy God

B-7644 {Hebrew Children in the Fiery Furnace
He Was Born in a Manger

B-7758 {Death's Black Train Is Comin'
Yonder Comes My Lord With a Bible in His Hand

B-7936 {Somebody's Been Stealing
Kidnapping

B-8038 {The Racket Train— Parts 1 and 2

B-8108 {This Heart of Mine— Parts 1 and 2

B-8148 {So Glad I'm Here in Jesus' Name— Parts 1 and 2

B-8256 {Baptist World Alliance in Atlanta, Georgia
Hell Without Fire

B-8301 {Will Hell Be Your Santa Claus?
Smoking Woman on the Street

B-8382 {Men and Women Talk Too Much
Joe Louis' Wrist and His Fist

GEORGIA WASHBOARD STOMPERS

B-5092 {Nobody's Sweetheart—FT—VR
Bug-A-Boo—FT

Jazz GILLUM and his Jazz Boys

B-6445 {Sarah Jane
I Want You By My Side

B-7341 {Alberta Blues
Birmingham Blues

B-7563 {Gillum's Windy Blues
Boar Hog Blues

B-8189 {Against My Will
Big Katy Adams

B-8221 {Keyhole Blues
Talking to Myself

B-8257 {One Time Blues
Somebody Been Talking to You

B-8287 {Hard Drivin' Woman
Got to Reap What You Sow

GOLDEN GATE JUBILEE QUARTET Records
(Male voices unaccompanied)

B-7126 {Golden Gate Gospel Train
Gabriel Blows His Horn

B-7154 {Jonah
Behold the Bridegroom Cometh

B-7205 {Preacher and the Bear
Born Ten Thousand Years Ago

B-7264 {Bonnet
Massa's in the Cold, Cold Ground

B-7278 {Bedside of a Neighbor
Found a Wonderful Saviour

B-7340 {Go Where I Send Thee
Won't There Be One Happy Time

B-7376 {Job
Stand in the Test in Judgment

B-7415 {Dipsy Doodle
Carolina in the Morning

B-7617 {Take Your Burdens to God
Lead Me On and On

B-7631 {John, the Revelator
See How They Done My Lord (Evening Song)

B-7848 {God Almighty Said
Bye and Bye Little Children

B-7897 {When They Ring the Golden Bells
Saints Go Marching In

B-7994 {What Are They Doing in Heaven Today?
Lord, Am I Born to Die?

B-8019 {Cheer the Weary Traveler
Packing Up—Getting Ready to Go

B-8123 {Lis'n to de Lambs
Dese Bones Gonna Rise Agin

B-8160 {This World Is in a Bad Condition
Noah

B-8306 {Way Down in Egypt Land
If I Had My Way

B-8328 {Every Time That I Feel the Spirit
He Said He Would Calm the Ocean

25

A page from the 1940 Bluebird catalogue. B5033 and B5111 by Rev Gates were reissues of early Victor material; B5627 to B5901 were recorded in Atlanta in 1934; B7644 to B7936 were again reissues of titles originally made between 1926 and 1928; the final six records had been recorded in 1939. The Golden Gate quartet also accompanied Leadbelly on six sides, issued on the expensive Victor label in 1940.

Top: *Walter Davis, right, and Sonny Boy Williamson, left, were mainstays of the Bluebird race list.*

And two fine country blues singers were dug out by the talent scouts. Bukka White had made fourteen sides, of which only four were ever issued, for Victor in Memphis in 1930; and then – through Lester Melrose – two for Vocalion in Chicago in 1937. White's intense throaty singing and driving guitar appealed to black record buyers and Vocalion asked him to return to make some more titles; but by then he had been committed to the Mississippi State Penitentiary. It wasn't until Melrose secured his parole in 1940 that he was able to travel north and record twelve more numbers, mostly blues about prison life. CBS paid him well, by their standards: $17.50 per selection, and $20 overall for accompanist Washboard Sam; with $33.50 payment for expenses the twelve tunes cost the company $263.50.

In November 1939 Bluebird recorded Tommy McClennan, a Mississippi singer with a gravelly voice and primitive but effective guitar accompaniment; he was immediately in demand, and had eight records issued in 1941. At McClennan's last session, in

Bottom: *The first four records on this page from December 1941 Bluebird catalogue are by 'Huddie Leadbelly'. B10177, by Little Brother Montgomery and Pinetop and Lindberg Sparks, had been issued in the pop series in the hope that it would appeal to the white market.*

February 1942, he recorded *Bluebird Blues,* issued on Bluebird B9037, a plea to the company to come and ask him to do some more recording:

Bluebird, Bluebird, please fly right down to me (*twice*)
If you don't find me on the M & O, you'll find me on the
Santa Fe

B-8570 { Easy Rider
        { Worried Blues
B-8709 { Roberta
        { The Red Cross Store Blues
B-8750 { New York City
        { You Can't Lose-a Me Cholly
B-8791 { Good Morning Blues
        { Leaving Blues

HARLAN LEONARD and his Orchestra
—See Leonard in Popular Catalog

LITTLE BROTHER
B-10177 { East Chicago Blues
        {   (Pinetop and Lindberg)
        { Farish Street Jive

ROBERT LOCKWOOD
(Blues singer with instrumental acc.)
B-8820 { Little Boy Blue
        { Take a Little Walk with Me

TOMMY McCLENNAN (Singing with guitar)
B-8347 { You Can
        { Mistreat
        { Me Here
        { New "Shake
        { 'Em on
        { Down"
B-8373 { Whiskey
        { Head
        { Woman
        { Bottle It Up
        { and Go
B-8408 { Baby, Don't·
        { You Want
        { to Go?
        { Cotton
        { Patch
        { Blues
B-8444 { Brown Skin Girl
        { Baby, Please Don't Tell on Me
B-8499 { New Highway No. 51
        { I'm Goin', Don't You Know
B-8545 { My Baby's Doggin' Me
        { She's a Good Looking Mama
B-8605 { She's Just Good Huggin' Size
        { My Little Girl
B-8669 { My Baby's Gone
        { It's Hard to Be Lonesome
B-8689 { Katy Mae Blues
        { Love With a Feeling
B-8704 { Black Minnie
        { Drop Down Mama
B-8725 { Elsie Blues
        { Down to Skin and Bones
B-8760 { Whiskey Head Man—Blues
        { New Sugar Mama—Blues

ROBERT LEE McCOY
B-7440 { C N A
        { Want to Woogie Some More—FT
        {   —VR (Washboard Sam's Band)

REV. F. W. McGEE Sermons
B-5261 { Jonah in the Belly of the Whale
        { Babylon Is Falling Down
B-5345 { Nothing to Do in Hell
        { Fifty Miles of Elbow Room

McKINNEY'S COTTON PICKERS—See
McKinney's Cotton Pickers in
Popular Catalog

MEMPHIS SLIM
B-8584 { Beer
        { Drinking
        { Woman
        { Grinder
        { Man
        { Blues
B-8615 { Empty
        { Room
        { Blues
        { You Didn't
        { Mean Me
        { No Good
B-8645 { I See My
        { Great
        { Mistake
        { Shelby
        { County
        { Blues
B-8749 { Jasper's Gal
        { Two of a Kind
B-8784 { Maybe I'll Lend You a Dime
        { Me, Myself and I
B-8834 { Whiskey Store Blues
        { You Got to Help Me Some

The MISSOURIANS
B-6084 { Scotty Blues—FT
        { Tiger Rag—FT
        {   (Washboard Rhythm Kings)

CLARA MORRIS
(Blues singer with piano and guitar)
B-8700 { I'm Blue,
        { Daddy
        { I Stagger
        { In My
        { Sleep
B-8767 { Poker
        { Playing
        { Daddy
        { Cry On,
        { Daddy

END OF AN ERA   1941-1945

The race labels had always kept considerable quantities of old issues in catalogue. One of the longest-lived records was the Norfolk Jubilee Quartet's *Father Prepare Me* and *My Lord's Gonna Move This Wicked Race*, issued on Paramount 12035 in mid-1923 and still available when the company folded nine years later. Sales were so great that the original masters wore out, and the Quartet was called back at least once to re-record the titles. Even through the depression years large catalogues were maintained. The 1935 Vocalion catalogue listed every record put out by Memphis Minnie and all but one of the forty-six items by Leroy Carr; most of these were in the Vocalion 1000 series, originally priced at 75 cents, but now available for only 35 cents. Victor did not reduce the price of any records, preferring instead to start a new label, Bluebird. Victor race issues were withdrawn and only a few of them reissued on the cheaper label, but the company kept most Bluebird blues around for a fair time – the 1937 catalogue listed 175 currently available blues and gospel discs. Decca, however, went one better and declared that *all* their issues would remain permanently available; according to the 1940 catalogue it was still possible to buy every record put out in the 7000 series since it began in 1934.

In the late 'thirties there were no large advertisements, or supplements with lurid drawings telling the story of a blues; no way-out copy impressing upon the customer that he could not afford to be without such-and-such a record. The companies merely listed the new releases – blues coming after hillbilly in the supplements – with specification of the instrumentation. Decca issued separate race catalogues, whereas BRC-ARC listed race records in a final section of the general catalogue. Victor had admitted hillbilly into the general catalogue in 1933, but excluded records by black artists. In 1937 the Bluebird catalogue mingled all types of music with only the pictures of some of the artists in a centre section showing their colour. However, by the end of the 'thirties there was a separate Bluebird catalogue for non-pop items: the first section dealt with hillbilly (under the name Old Familiar Tunes), then came Race Records, followed by Children's, Cajun and finally Irish items.

From 1934 on the three companies had played fairly equal parts in supplying black record enthusiasts. Then, in 1941, with industry sales once more topping a hundred million discs, there was a further cut-back in race releases; Bluebird still put out 100 new items but Decca and Columbia, for the first time in five years, fell well short of the figure. That year several Decca artists moved company – Roosevelt Sykes to Columbia, and Johnnie Temple and Sleepy John Estes to Bluebird.

Early in 1942 the government restricted the use of shellac, and blues and gospel releases – at 125 – were half what they had been in '41. Well over half of these came from Victor, with Washboard Sam still the firm favourite, followed by Tampa Red, Walter Davis, Sonny Boy Williamson and Tommy McClennan. Columbia released only a score or so race items on their OKeh label (the renamed Vocalion), and a third of these were by Big Bill. Decca's main activity surrounded Blind Boy Fuller – the issue of material recorded five years earlier – and the Selah Jubilee Singers.

In July 1942 the president of the American Federation of Musicians, J. C. Petrillo – worried about the effects of jukeboxes on live music – announced a ban on all recording, and the studios were closed for two years. But race material that had already been recorded remained unissued by and large, and the catalogues were ruthlessly pruned. The December 1941 Victor catalogue listed 350 blues and gospel items, whereas in May 1943 there were only seventy-five items available, and only two of these had been issued before 1940 – Washboard Sam's *Diggin' My Potatoes* from 1939, and his still-popular *Back Door*, from '37.

Between 1920 and 1942 about 5,500 blues and 1,250 gospel records had been issued, involving all told about 1,200 artists. Two performers – Tampa Red and Big Bill – each had more than 100 releases; sixteen more had between fifty and a hundred and a further fifty-four between twenty and fifty; these seventy-two most popular artists altogether accounted for almost half the total releases.

Although commercial recording of music came to a standstill with the Petrillo ban, one recording concern was unaffected – the Music Division of the Library of Congress. Since 1933 they had been collecting all types of folk music on record to form a permanent reference library in their Archives. A dedicated group of researchers, led by John A. Lomax, had been combing the countryside with small mobile recording units, concentrating particularly on prison farms and penitentiaries. Over the course of the nine years up to 1942 they had recorded about 4,000 titles by at least 850 black singers, quite apart from their activities in hillbilly and other spheres.

The blues and ballad singer Huddie Ledbetter – better known as Leadbelly – was discovered and recorded by Lomax in the State Penitentiary, Angola, Louisiana, in 1933, and after his release continued to record for them right up to his death in 1949. In May 1939 Library of Congress field workers stumbled upon Bukka White in the State Penitentiary at Parchman, Mississippi, where he was serving a sentence for shooting a man and recorded just two titles, *Po' Boy* and *Sic 'Em Dogs On*. In 1940 Blind Willie McTell bobbed up in Atlanta – recording activity seemed to draw him like a magnet – and recorded a long series of songs Paramount days, and, realising what they had found, the re-1941 unearthed the magnificent Son House, unrecorded since his and reminiscences. A trip to Lake Cormorant. Mississippi in searchers returned again in 1942 for more. One might say their star discovery, however, was a young country boy called McKinley Morganfield whom they recorded in Stovall, Mississippi, in 1941 and 1942. He was soon to be known to the public as Muddy Waters and to be one of the most commercially successful blues singers of the post-war period.

Before leaving the war years, two companies who played their own small part in blues recording history should not be overlooked. The first, appearing in 1939, was Varsity, the product of one-time Victor executive Eli Oberstein. The label was intended as a competitor to the big three – Bluebird, Vocalion and Decca – and Oberstein immediately instituted a race series. This began with a number of reissues of Paramount material through an arrangement with the Crown label, which had been connected with Paramount in the early 'thirties. This soon changed to Gennett material, either by arrangement with Harry Gennett himself, or through Decca who had acquired rights in 1935 when buying Champion. Almost all issues were under simple-minded pseudonyms – Sally Sad, Tall Tom, Big Boy Ben, Jim Jam and others. The name Down South Boys concealed the identity of the Mississippi Sheiks on Varsity 6009, and of preacher Black Billy Sunday and the Norfolk Jubilee Quartet on either side of 6011. However, a general lowering of prices by Victor and Columbia in mid-1940 precipitated Oberstein into bankruptcy and by autumn 1941, after reissuing some of the rarest Champions of the depression years, the Varsity race series had disappeared.

The second label was Joe Davis, produced towards the end of

the war by the music publisher, singer and promoter of the 'twenties of that name, who first attempted to revive the old Gennett label. Although Harry Gennett had ceased making records for the public in 1934, he had continued with private work such as sound effects for radio stations. Joe Davis made a deal whereby he obtained Gennett's war-time shellac ration in return for loaning Gennett a lot of money to refurbish his pressing plant. Gennett sold him pressings for 20 cents each plus .02 cents excise tax, old Electrobeam sleeves were used for the records, and the legend 'Gennett Record Division, The Starr Piano Co Inc, Richmond, Indiana' appeared on the label. 1930

Wonder Where's The Gamblin' Man, by the Norfolk Jubilee Quartet, was originally issued on Paramount 12715 in 1927, reissued on Paramount 13150 in 1932 and then on Crown 3328 before turning up pseudonymously on Varsity in 1939.

RACE
ENTERTAINMENT

Small wonder that Victor were elbowed out of the race market by the new companies that sprang up in the late forties when one sees the illustrations that opened (above) and closed (right) the 'Race' section of the 1943 general catalogue. Five years later its catalogue had no separate race section, and just 33 blues records were included in the general list, including two by Walter Davis, three by Roosevelt Sykes and four by Tampa Red.

rarities by artists such as Big Bill and Georgia Tom appeared, plus newly recorded items by an artist in no way connected with Gennett: Gabriel Brown (he had been recorded in Florida in 1935 by the Library of Congress).

The idea of a Gennett revival was dropped after eight issues and the label name changed to Joe Davis. More titles by Gabriel Brown appeared together with some by pianist Champion Jack Dupree and by Columbia's Rev J. C. Burnett. By now Davis had acquired Oberstein's Varsity masters, but, apparently deciding that race records no longer paid, the venture soon drifted into other channels.

When the Petrillo ban ended in 1944 the big companies made a half-hearted attempt to carry on as before. A new Bluebird race series had been begun in 1943 and Decca and Columbia soon followed suit. Victor continued with their old favourites Washboard Sam, Tampa Red and Sonny Boy Williamson, and Columbia with Memphis Minnie and Big Bill; Decca had no big-name blues singers left. But the public mood was changing, and with it the type of music people were prepared to pay for. Sensing this, a number of small record companies sprang up in all parts of the country – in Chicago, Detroit, the south, and the west coast – and were soon supplying public demand. Many of the new ventures were under black ownership. The large companies were swiftly left behind. When Victor discontinued the Bluebird label in 1950 they made sure to reissue Washboard Sam's two most successful tunes, *Back Door* and *Diggin' My Potatoes*, on Victor 20-2162. But these were now old and stale and not to be compared with, for example, the rousing, shouting, throbbing Muddy Waters records that were being put out by the emerging Chicago record company, Chess. It was an altogether new era in blues recording.

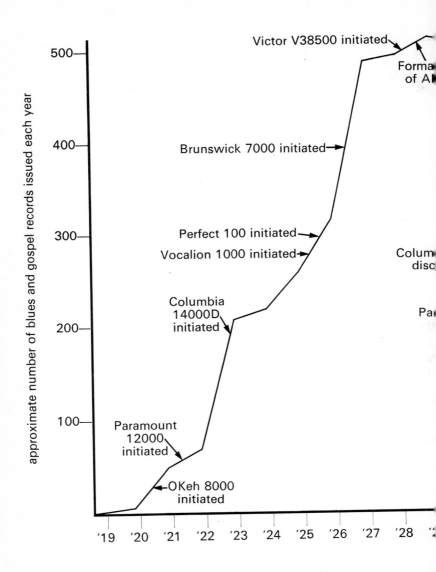

Graph showing approximate number o
and the extents o

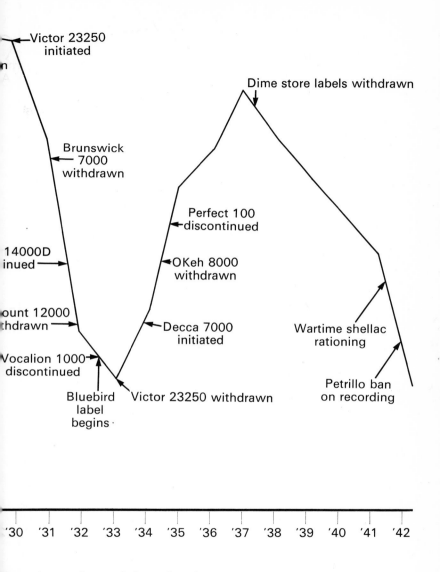

Victor 23250
initiated

Dime store labels withdrawn

Brunswick
7000
withdrawn

Perfect 100
discontinued

14000D
inued

OKeh 8000
withdrawn

ount 12000
thdrawn

Decca 7000
initiated

Wartime shellac
rationing

Vocalion 1000
discontinued

Victor 23250 withdrawn

Petrillo ban
on recording

Bluebird
label
begins

'30 '31 '32 '33 '34 '35 '36 '37 '38 '39 '40 '41 '42

es and gospel records issued each year
e major race series

Year	Atlanta, Georgia	Dallas and Fort Worth, Texas	Memphis, Tennessee	New Orleans, Louisiana	San Antonio, Texas
'23	OK				
'24	OK			OK	
'25	OK, Co			OK	
'26	OK, Co			Co	
'27	Co, Vi	Co	Co, Vi	Co, Vi	
'28	OK, Co, Vi, Vo	Co, Vo	OK, Vi, Vo	Co, Vo	OK
'29	OK, Co, Vi	Co, Vi, Vo	Vi, Vo	OK, Co, Vo	OK
'30	OK, Co, Vo	Vo	Vi, Vo		OK
'31	OK, Co				
'32	Vi	Vi			
'33					
'34	BB	Vo			
'35	BB	Vo		BB	
'36		Vo		De, BB	
'37		Vo			
'38		Vo			
'39	BB	Vo	Vo		
'40	BB	Vo			
'41	BB	BB			
'42					

CHART OF FIELD TRIPS

Under each town are shown the record labels which recorded blues and gospel material there, year by year. The following abbreviations are used:

BB – Bluebird   Co – Columbia   De – Decca
Ge – Gennett   OK – OKeh   Vi – Victor
Vo – Vocalion (recording jointly with the chain store labels in the mid-thirties)

	Birmingham, Alabama	Bristol, Tennessee	Charlotte, North Carolina	Jackson, Mississippi	Knoxville, Tennessee	Rock Hill, South Carolina	St Louis, Missouri	Other locations
							OK	
							OK	
							OK	
	Ge	Vi	Vi					Vi: Savannah, Ga
	Vo	Vi						Vi: Nashville, Tenn; Vo: Indianapolis, Ind
					Vo			OK: Richmond, Va; Co: Greensboro, N.C.; Vo: Kansas City, Kan
				OK	Vo			OK: Shreveport, La; Vi: Cincinnati, Ohio
			Vi					Vi: Louisville, Ky
Vo							Vo	
Vo				Vo				
Vo			BB					Vo: Augusta, Ga and Hattiesburg, Miss
Vo	Vo		BB					Vo: Hot Springs, Ark
						BB		Vo: Columbia, S.C.
						BB		

FURTHER READING

The Story Of The Blues by Paul Oliver (Barrie and Rockliff, London and Chilton Books, Philadelphia, 1969) provides a full survey of the origin and development of the blues, with several hundred pictures, many of which also illustrate points in the present book. Paul Oliver's *Screening The Blues* (Cassell, 1968) discusses the relationship between blues and gospel music, and investigates gambling, protest and sexual themes in blues. In *The Bluesmen* (Oak Publications, New York, 1967) Samuel B. Charters tells of the lives and music of some of the great singers from Mississippi, Alabama and Texas. *Blues And Gospel Records, 1902–1942* by John Godrich and Robert M. W. Dixon (revised edition 1969, Storyville Publications, 63 Orford Road, London E.17) is a comprehensive 912-page listing of all recordings of the period, with an appendix on microgroove reissues and thumb-nail sketches of the major race labels. There are two first-class studies of individual race series: *The Columbia 13/14000D Series* by Dan Mahoney (published by Walter C. Allen, Stanhope, New Jersey, 1961) and *The Paramount 12/13000 Series* by Max E. Vreede (scheduled from Storyville Publications, 1970). Also scheduled for 1970 publication is an excellent study by Ronald C. Foreman, Jnr, *Jazz and Race Records, 1920–32; Their Origins And Their Significance For The Record Industry And Society* (Louisiana State University Press). For a general account of the development of the record industry the reader is recommended to *The Fabulous Phonograph* by Roland Gelatt (Cassell, 1956).

ACKNOWLEDGMENTS

The information contained in this book has been collected from many sources over a period of fifteen or so years; it would be impossible to list all those who have helped us. Special thanks are due to Walter C. Allen, Helene Chmura (late of Columbia Records), Derek Coller, E. C. Foreman (of RCA-Victor), Robert G. Koester, John K. MacKenzie, Dan Mahony, Paul Oliver, Tony Russell, Brian Rust, Max Vreede, Bert Whyatt and Bob Yates. Paul Oliver, Bert Whyatt and Bob Yates also read the initial draft of the book and made welcome suggestions and criticisms. Amongst our published sources are the books mentioned in the Further Reading section, Michael Wyler's *A Glimpse At The Past*, and the magazines *Record Research*, *Jazz Journal* and *Record Changer*.

ACCOMPANYING RECORD

Lucille Bogan: *Skin Game Blues*. Bertha 'Chippie' Hill (with Louis Armstrong): *Kid Man Blues*. Blind Lemon Jefferson: *Rabbit Foot Blues*. Whistlin' Alex Moore: *Blue Bloomer Blues*. Barbecue Bob: *Crooked Woman Blues*. Georgia Cotton Pickers: *She's Coming Back Some Cold Rainy Day*. Rev. J. M. Gates: *Death's Black Train Is Coming*. Mississippi Sheiks: *Loose Like That*. Blind Willie Johnson: *When The War Was On*. Allen Shaw: *I Couldn't Help It*. Robert Wilkins: *New Stock Yard Blues*. Bumble Bee Slim: *Bricks In My Pillow*. Big Bill: *Detroit Special*. Lil Johnson: *Press My Button (Ring My Bell)*. Peetie Wheatstraw: *Ain't It A Pity And A Shame*. Pinetop Burks: *Fannie Mae Blues*.

INDEX

Italic indicates publications and books, while page numbers in italic indicate mention in the graph, and in illustration and illustration captions. Small capitals indicates record label names; boldface type indicates key pages.